Hidden Treasures
of
Ancient American
Cultures

Hidden Treasures
of
Ancient American Cultures

by

John Heinerman

Bonneville Books
Springville, Utah

ISBN: 1-55517-519-8
v.2

Published by Bonneville Books
Imprint of Cedar Fort Inc.

Distributed by:

BONNEVILLE BOOKS™

Typeset by Virginia Reeder
Cover design by Adam Ford
Cover design © 2001 by Lyle Mortimer

Printed in the United States of America
10 9 8 7 6 5 4 3 2 1

Printed on acid-free paper

Dedicated To

APOSTLE ORSON PRATT,

"The St. Paul of Mormonism."

(Edward W. Tullidge, The History of Salt Lake City
and Its Founders; Salt Lake City: Edward W.
Tullidge, Publisher, 1886; p.32)

TABLE OF CONTENTS

FOREWORD

The ancient history of America has been somewhat of an enigma for those early Spanish and Portuguese explorers, and British, French, and Dutch emigrants who colonized different sections of the New world, following the discovery of the Americas by Cristobal Colon in 1492. Fear, awe, and much speculation ensued with the findings of many excavated mounds and explored caves over the succeeding centuries, a number of which contained many curious artifacts of fine craftsmanship, most of which were usually accompanied with the presence of gigantic skeletons measuring between eight and nine feet in length.

For the first time, a sensibly-written book on such a thrilling theme has been produced, which brings together the more significant accounts of these past discoveries. And uses The Book of Mormon as a standard reference guide towards giving Mormon and non-LDS readers alike a background history of such unusual findings, that is both reasonable and very possible. Additional references are incorporated as well, that range from apocryphal writings and antiquated histories to scientific books devoted exclusively to ancient cultures in both the Old as well as New Worlds. Extensive use is also made of statements made by leading men of the early Mormon Church, such as Joseph Smith, Brigham young, Orson Pratt, George Reynolds, and others, who shed new light on such little-known matters.

There is a sore need for such a volume as this to help check the wildly extravagant claims made by various treasure-hunting books on the one hand, and the uncomfortably starched, closely-defined opinions of said scholars on the other. Somewhere in between a balance, has been struck with the views expressed in this book, the author hopes. Nevertheless, he knows that members of the scholastic community will surely take potshots at some of the things advanced here. But since "truth is in the heart of the beholder," the author fully recognizes that some of the proud and learned academics will surely put down some of the conclusions made here as being utterly ridiculous or entirely without merit. However, the common logic to be found in such things will definitely appeal to all those whose mind and hearts have not been thoroughly corrupted or prejudiced with that kind of jaundiced skepticism so consistent with modern education.

The world before the Flood is a recurring theme throughout the text, because the author feels it is paramount to understanding more about the original settlers of the Western Hemisphere—the Jaredites who came over to this part of the world from the Great Tower then being erected in what is now southern Iraq. This same reference to the Antediluvians also helps us to better understand the organization of the Gadianton Robbers, a widespread criminal fraternity of Book of Mormon times.

This author's own personal involvement in things of antiquity is delineated here for the very first time over a number of different chapters. While obviously controversial in nature and sure to garner the scorn of some professional archaeologists and other educators, it is likely to inspire, hopefully for good purposes, many other readers who lead honorable but mundane lives. For them, this book is guaranteed to take some of the boredom away and replace it with an adrenal excitement inspired by true things.

I knew a long time ago that someday such a book would need to be written, but always held off out of concern for the lightning controversy and many brush-fire criticisms that it would indeed engender. But I've had several good decades filled with much honor and good will from many, many people who've been helped by a number of my fairly normal alternative health publications. The time has now come for such a work as this, to set before men and women everywhere, valuable information concerning the ancient lives and cultures of some of America's former inhabitants, as this author understands them to be.

–Your good friend, John Heinerman, September 2000.

CHAPTER ONE

ACTION IN THE DESERT: THE ARIZONA FINDINGS

Shortly after his First Vision experience with God and Christ in the Sacred Grove near Palmyra, New York, which forever transformed the face of American religion, young Joseph Smith, the founder of Mormonism, acquired his first seerstone by using someone else's "peepstone." He was about fourteen at the time when he looked into the borrowed stone, and according to Brigham Young, "[saw the other one] in an iron kettle 25 feet underground [and] went right to the spot & dug & found it" (Wilford Woodruff's Journal 5:382-83 under the entry for September 11th, 1859). This first seerstone was whitish and opaque and found in September 1819. His second seerstone came from a well for the Chase family in Palmyra sometime in 1822 and "was green with brown, irregular spots on it." Of the two, it had more peculiar powers and was favored the most by the young teenager. For the next several years, he engaged himself in numerous treasure digging activities, sometimes with other male members of his own family (such as his father and brothers) or neighbors. Eventually he joined a group of professional treasure hunters and, because of his seership abilities, became their point man in locating such things. Quite often he was paid for his services and this extra income greatly supplemented the Smith family's own struggling finances. A non-LDS scholar, friendly to the Mormon cause, Jan Shipps, was of the opinion that Joseph's many treasure-digging episodes, instead of being harmful, were actually beneficial to him and "played an important role in his spiritual development" for translating the Book of Mormon a few years later (see D. Michael Quinn's Early Mormonism and the Magic World View, Revised and Enlarged (Salt Lake City: Signature Books, 1998; pp. 43-46;63-64); and BYU Studies 24(4):412-413 (Fall 1986).

But a good look at real treasures came for Joseph, Jr., his father Joseph Smith, Sr. and Oliver Cowdery when they went to the Hill Cumorah one time. The Journal of James E. Talmage (3:151-152; Special Collections, Lee Library, BYU), under the entry date of August 14th, 1890, recorded the episode in full.

"On the way home father related to me the following incident as told [to] by Hiram Winters shortly before his death. Father Smith, the Prophet's father, came once to Hiram Winter's house while the latter was suffering a slight despondency caused by the poverty-stricken condition (with respect to worldly riches) in which he and all others of the Church found themselves. To cheer Bro. Winters spirits, Father Smith assured him that the Church did not really lack money, that there were tons of gold stored away which he himself had seen. He said he had accompanied his son Joseph, the Prophet, and Oliver Cowdery. Joseph had been commanded to take the [Gold] Plates again to the Hill Cumorah...after the translation of the Book of Mormon had been completed...As to the further disposition of them, neither he nor his companions knew anything till they arrived at the Hill. Then they saw an opening like a tunnel on the hillside. At its entrance stood a personage who beckoned them in. All entered, and soon found them-selves in a spacious room, within which was a table bearing a number of books of plates, resembling the Book of Mormon plates. Some of these the elders were permitted to read, and the gift of interpretation was given to each [so] that he fully understood the characters [before him]. In the room were piles of gold, mostly or all in bars of different lengths, and each stamped as if once used as a coin. A sword that had hung over the door as they entered was now taken down by the angelic personage in charge, and was placed upon the table, unsheathed, except [for] its top. Upon its blade the elders read: 'This, the sword of Laban, shall never more be sheathed till the kingdoms of this earth become the kingdoms of our Lord.' The brethren were then conducted to the entrance [of] the tunnel, and turning round they saw only the continuous hill surface."

Such riches as those which once were in Cumorah were undoubtedly consecrated a long time ago unto God and for the building up of His kingdom on earth when the Devil's own kingdom is finally supplanted and the full redemption of Zion takes place. But there are caves and tombs all over the land in which different kinds of

2

treasures have been secreted for a very, very long time. Some of the more spectacular finds (including a fabulous one in which the author of this book himself participated) are mentioned in detail here. In a sense they help to set a precedent for what follows in succeeding chapters. Because while this book may be about "hidden records" and treasures (as the title obviously implies), it also is something about those "ancient American cultures" (the rest of the title) to whom such riches belonged.

While the bulk of Cumorah's untold treasures may belong to the Nephites (an extinct Book of Mormon culture), the astounding mummies and artifacts you will be learning about here were all connected with an even older Book of Mormon civilization known as the Jaredites. They originally emigrated from the Tower of Babel, believed to have been located about fifty-five miles south of present Baghdad, the capitol of Iraq. They came by way of this distinctive name after one of their leaders, a man named Jared, who with his brother, were instrumental in gathering together a rather large tribe of family, friends, and acquaintances, and relocating them to the shores of the Western Hemisphere following partial destruction of the tower itself and the changing of a universally common language, which everyone then spoke, into numerous dialects which very few could understand. We know they came from that place because of what the Book of Mormon (Ether 1:33) says, as well as some lineal evidence: Kish is the name given to one of the old Jaredite kings (Ether 1:18-19). But it goes back even further into antiquity than this: "Kish was the seat of the first Sumerian dynasty after the Flood" (located not far from the later Babylon, just a little to the southeast), not to mention the name given to the first dynasty of Sumerian kings (see Jack Finnegan's Light From the Ancient Past (Princeton, NJ: Princeton University Press, 1946; pp. 11;24;31).

We also know that the Jaredites brought with them huge elephants, as they are mentioned only once in that part of the Book of Mormon covering these people (Ether 9:19). The Sumerians, who helped initiate the building of the Great Tower in the Old world, also kept big elephants around to help with the very heavy work (see Henry Frederick Lutz', Sumerian Temple Records of The Late Ur Dynasty (Berkeley, CA: University of California Press, 1928; pp. 153-55).

Another identifying characteristic of these people from the

Great Tower is their enormous size and immense physical strength: "And the brother of Jared being a LARGE AND MIGHTY MAN" (Ether 1:34). When the Spaniards under Hernan Cortez entered the territory and principal Indian city of Tlascala on September 23rd, 1519, they were given a royal welcome by the nation's head chiefs. A soldier-historian by the name of Captain Bernal Diaz del Castillo was one of the army officers present with Cortez when they met with their hosts. As he later recorded in his True History of The Conquest of Mexico (London: John Dean, 1800; pp. 113-14) "The Tlascalan chiefs said that their ancestors had told them, that in former times the country was inhabited by men and women of great stature, and wicked manners, whom their ancestors had at length extirpated. And in order that we might judge of the bulk of these people, they brought us a bone which had belonged to one of them. [It was] so large, that when placed upright it was as high as a middling-sized man; it was the bone between the knee and the hip. I stood by it, and it was of my height, though I am as tall as the generality of men. They brought also pieces of other bones of great size, but much consumed by time. But the one I have mentioned was entire. We were astonished by these remains, and thought that they certainly demonstrated the former existence of giants."

The great Aztec poet Nezahualcoyotl captured the final end of this race of American giants in one of his poems: "The caverns of earth are filled with pestilential dust which was once bones, the flesh, the bodies of the GREAT ONES who sat upon thrones, deciding causes, ruling assemblies, governing armies, conquering provinces, possessing treasures, tearing down temples, flattering themselves with pride, majesty, fortune, praise and dominion. [But] these glories have passed like the dark smoke thrown out by the fires of [the volcano] Popocatepetl, leaving no monument of these giants" (see George Creel's The People Next Door (New York: John Day Co., 1926; p. 15).

Each of the fascinating tomb discoveries, cited here in considerable detail, probably belongs to the ancient Jaredites by virtue of the HUGE skeletal remains or GIGANTIC mummies found therein, along with untold riches and strange artifacts of exceedingly fine workmanship and curious design. The states of Arizona, Ohio, and Utah (in that order) all seem to have a wonderful proclivity for such incredible finds.

To begin this thrilling journey back into the distant past when

4

gold was as common as credit cards are today, we first give some consideration to what was found down Tucson way. On March 3rd, 1757, this city was founded by a German friar named Father Bernard Middendorf, who spoke Spanish and was equally fluent in some of the Indian tongues of the American Southwest. One of the local Native Americans, who had been properly Christianized from his "wicked heathen ways" by the good padre, invited him along one particular time to inspect the odd contents of a certain cave, in which it was alleged lay "monstrous bodies of human form, and much riches" with them.

The Jesuit rode on a burro while the native trotted beside him, as was befitting a man of the cloth in those times. They traveled for some distance into wilderness country full of cacti until they reached a very remote canyon with high rock walls on both sides. The priest dismounted and he and the Indian paused to drink some water and rest a bit. They then moved towards one of the recesses or clefts in the cliff wall.

What looked like a small door was cut into the rock face, but could be opened and closed with some skill and strength. The guide motioned to the padre to help him push against one side of this door, which slid open a few inches with their combined efforts. Both men inched their way into the blackness of an interior man-made chamber of some size and dimension. The indian again motioned for Father Middendorf to lean with him against another part of the stone door, which then swung open more easily by several feet.

The priest was intrigued by the arrangement of this door and inspected it more closely. What he found was truly ingenious to say the least. The single stone slab which covered the entranceway had been fashioned to accommodate the hewn rock entry. This slab was several feet thick and quite tall. But the interesting part had to do with its most unusual suspension—it was held in an upright position with a very stout and long juniper pole that ran through a hole previously bored into the slab from top to bottom. Notches had been chiselled out in the rock overhead and beneath to hold the rounded ends of this thick, sturdy pole. The padre had never seen anything like it in his life—here was a swinging stone door held in place with a timbered pivot!

Sunlight now streamed into the chamber revealing its long-hidden surprises. A number of niches made into the smooth walls

5

contained large stone caskets, obviously weighing around a thousand pounds, covered with ornately carved stone lids and sealed with a dry, waxy substance that resembled melted honeycomb. One of the crypts had already been disturbed in that its lid had been pried loose and was laying in several broken pieces on the floor. Inside lay the mummified, resin-covered remains of an ancient-looking man of "monstrous size." A piece of decorated fabric covered the corpse from just below the chin to the abdomen. Reaching over to handle the material, the priest discovered that the fabric had a silky feel to it.

Father Bernard then put his hand down into the casket at which time the Indian let out a gasp of horror, imagining this to be a terrible act of desecrating the dead. The padre's fingers touched something cold and hard which was lifted out for closer examination. The object turned out to be a small horse with a single spiral horn coming out of the middle of its head, that was beautifully carved out of marble-like stone. Unfortunately, the priest's prejudice towards things he considered to be heathen idols overruled common sense and better judgment; consequently he threw the object against the wall, smashing it to pieces while in the process of venting his spleen. In the report he later filed with his superiors in Mexico City, the Jesuit admitted destroying this, as well as several other objects, giving as the absurd reason that "unicorns and dragons are the devil's work" and never existed!

His relation or lengthy letter also spoke of unspecified treasures that would be "worthy of a king's ransom." He also made mention of numerous weapons laying about, that included "long, broad swords of such weight, it took my guide and I [together] to lift one [of them], and of unsurpassed craftsmanship." He assumed from seeing such things that "these monsters must have been war-like in their habits." An uncomfortable feeling crept over him "and I imagined myself in purgatory with the unbaptized souls of those about me," his prejudicial fears influenced him to write. "We very quickly went out on my orders after securing the heavy stone door in place again, and I made the Indian swear before all that is sacred in our most holy church [that] he would return no more to this 'graveyard of the wicked,'" nor bring anyone else with him. Whatever became of this secret mountain tomb with its mysterious mummies and curious ancient treasures is anybody's guess. There is no official record anywhere of others going there later in hopes of relocating it. Perhaps, as the good friar himself concluded in his penned narrative, "It is the will of God that no one goes to this place of evil." (Father Bernard Middendorf's Relation de las indias de Visita de San Javier del Bac is in the Mexican Jesuit Archives in Mexico City, Mexico. I am grateful to the late Hector Rosales for calling this interesting document to my attention some years ago and providing the valuable translation services that made the inclusion of this part here possible.)

The next incredible find, this one also from somewhere near Tucson, AZ, was published in The Latter-day Saints' Millenial Star (53(14):235-36; April 13, 1891). "While removing earth for the foundation of a new hotel to be erected by Harmon & Brooks of this city [formerly Crittenden, Arizona], there was discovered what seems to be the tomb of a king, though of what people it would doubtless puzzle an antiquarian to say.

"The workmen had penetrated, at some eight feet below the surface of the ground, what they took to be a stone of soft, friable nature, but which was evidently masonry of superior workmanship, when they reached the tomb itself. This was composed of large square blocks of stone, which were identified as red or rose granite, and cemented together with such skill as to at first cause the whole, measuring twelve by fifteen feet, to appear as a solid mass. The opening of this, while very difficult, as the use of power was prohibited by Mr. Hendrickson, who, as a learned archaeologist, was placed in charge of the exhumation by the authorities, was accomplished by night, when the interest and curiosity of the party was so great that the work was continued by lamp light till dawn.

"The tomb when opened was found to contain a gigantic image of a man lying at full length and made of clay mixed with a sort of preparation which gives it a bright blue color and a slight elasticity, the whole appearing to have been subject to great heat. The image represents the naked figure, except for a very tight girdle about the waist, a pair of close-fitting sandals, and a crown on the head shaped very much like a bishop's mitre, but topped with the head of a hawk or eagle.

"The features are roughly molded, are of an imperious cast, and of a man in middle age, with a prominent nose and a very large mouth, but with cheekbones so low as to preclude all idea that the original could have been an Indian. The hands, which are as small as a woman's, and bear on the backs the head of the bird, as on the crown, are crossed on the breast, and hold an image about three inches long of a squatting figure, probably that of a god. The feet are also crossed, the right presenting the peculiarity of possessing a sixth toe, which the sandal is cut to bring into prominence, as if the owner had prided himself on it. The hair on the image is dressed in thick curls on both sides of the head, reaching to the shoulders, and brought down to the brows over the forehead.

"Careful examination of this clay figure revealed that it was merely the elaborate coffin of the real body, and could be opened from the back. This was done with all possible care, so as not to disturb the remains within. But a few handfuls of dust, dark brown and almost impalpable powder, is all that was left of the body. The crown, however, together with the girdle, the image of the god, and a large battle-axe with a blade of sharp glass or obsidian, and a handle of petrified wood, were found in the coffin.

"The crown is thick red gold, carved with minute but well-executed drawings representing battle scenes, triumphal marches, and other pictures, the meaning of which is somewhat misty. But in all [of these images] the principal figure is that of a man with six toes on his right foot. The workmanship of the whole crown is very fine, and the bird's head on top is a masterpiece worthy of Cellini [a renowned Italian goldsmith and sculptor, 1500-1571]. It holds on its mouth a magnificent chalchuites, or green diamond, valued by the Aztecs, with some attempt at lapidification.

"The girdle found is composed of plates of gold arranged like scales, and very thin, so as to give with every movement of the wearer's body. On each of these plates, which is in half ellipse, is engraved a figure or hieroglyphic, conveying, however, no hint of their meanings in their form. The image of what is presumably a god is made of clay combined with the preparation spoken of before, and also burnt until thoroughly hardened. It represents a male being, seated on a pedestal in a squatting posture, its eyes squinting and grinning in a hideous mirth, while both hands are placed over the ears, as if to shut out sound.

"A peculiar thing about this image is that the hair is represented as hanging down its neck in one long plait like a Chinaman's.

The figure is hollow, but contained only one half a dozen small black pebbles, highly polished, and a somewhat larger stone of a dull gray hue. The coffin and these relics are now on exhibition at the court house, and are to be donated to the State Museum of History and Archaeology at Tucson. No clue of any value as to what race the remains are to be ascribed can be found. But it is probable that it was one ante-dating even the mount-builders, and superior to [it] in knowledge of masonry, sculpture, and the working of metals."

Another great Arizona discovery of about the same period (1892) was reported in the *Pheonix Herald* and is offered as further proof that the Jaredites inhabited this section of country in ancient times in greater abundance than hitherto imagined. The article concerned an old grizzled prospector named Andrew Pauly, who claimed to have discovered, while looking for some lost horses, a "most peculiar appearance of the rock face in one of the more remote cliff recesses," up which he had been searching for water. "It gave me the impression of the work of some human hand. It looked like a small door cut into the rock and again skillfully closed by some dusty material." Because he was too exhausted and thirsty at that particular time, he rode away without fully satisfying his curiosity.

But he returned some time later properly outfitted with a pick, shovel, rock hammer and cold chisel, a pry bar, and a coal-oil lantern. He succeeded in finding the object of his search after some diligent looking around in the area he last left. Closer inspection revealed a genuine piece of masonry in a cut opening in the solid rock. It was of such thickness and consistency that it took him five days with his tools to make an opening through the cement and rock that packed the entranceway, so a man his size could crawl in.

Prospector Pauly informed the journalist writing up his fabulous find that once he got inside, he found himself in a chamber apparently cut from solid rock not less than twenty by forty in dimensions and some ten feet high. The floor was covered with seven immense skeletons of men, who in life must have been not less than eight feet in height. There was additional evidence in there that they must have been great warriors because of the copper shields, copper spear heads, battle axes and other implements of war which were found with their remains.

One of the more interesting of those artifacts, not relating to warfare, was a small gold amulet with intricate design work on it. And while making his way to the end of the chamber, he stumbled across an opening that was closed with what seemed to be a type of heavy bronze door. It fit into the hewn rock entryway so snugly that it almost seemed like a part of the stone wall itself. Pauly estimated the door to be about two by three feet in dimensions and of considerable thickness. When he tabbed his rock hammer against it, though, there came forth a ringing echo in the distance indicating another room behind this burial chamber. The old prospector now became filled with excitement and determined to return again as soon as he could with the right kind of equipment for the removal of such a heavy bronze covering. He told the Herald representative that "he thinks he may be on to nothing less than a treasure vault of a very ancient royalty." That was the last time anyone saw or heard of Pauly ever again. The reporter covering his previous sojourns to this unidentified place was himself at a loss to know what happened to poor Pauly. Did his hidden treasure chamber finally do him in? Had one of the old Jaredite kings placed some kind of curse on the vault itself, that whomsoever dared venture into it would suffer irreversible consequences because of their greed? Was Pauly's tomb discovery similar to or, in fact, one-and-the-same made by Father Middendorf of Tucson with his Indian guide some 125 years earlier? Who knows or can say for sure, except that there still remains undiscovered a number of such hidden tombs located in out-of-the-way and hard-to-get places.

CHAPTER TWO

AN ASTONISHING FIND: THE OHIO CAVE BURIAL OF MUMMY GIANTS

As unique as those Arizona findings were, an even more attractive discovery was made in the 19th century in Adams County, Ohio and reported in the Cincinnati Commercial newspaper. The Mormon-owned *Deseret News*, ever on the prowl for good archaeological stories to support the Book of Mormon (in this case the book of Ether), promptly snapped the piece up and reprinted it for the benefit of its many LDS and some Gentile readers in the weekly edition of March 3, 1880 (29(5):73).

For in Adams County have been found not only bones of a gigantic race of men, but their implements of warfare and husbandry, and excellently preserved specimens of their art in sculpture, painting, engraving and writing.

"In conversation with some of the oldest citizens of this county, I have been enabled to learn the date of the discovery of a cave on the old Smith farm in Pitlin[?] township. Its existence was proven to the earliest settlers, and they probably learned of it from the Indians. For years it has been a place of resort for the curious and was always esteemed a great natural curiosity. The Smith farm is on the Portsmouth Pike, being 15 and 16 miles northeast of [Pitlin? Township]. The farm is a fertile, well-cultivated body of land.

"About one mile from the pike is a level plateau of 200 odd acres, surrounded on all sides by lofty hills. As you near the mouth of the cave, there is a gradual depression of the ground on every side, forming what, in the local nomenclature, is denominated a 'sink hole.' At the bottom of this circular basin is a hole three feet in diameter and about 25 feet in depth, at which distance from the top of the ground you strike the floor of the first chamber.

"In one corner of this chamber is an elevation, which, when

surmounted, discloses a yawning well, with a mouth ten feet in diameter, and of unknown depth. Apply your ear to the edge of the well and you can hear the hollow roaring of a stream of water hundreds of feet below. A few days ago a party of gentlemen visited the cave, provided with a plentiful supply of lanterns, ropes, and tools, for the purpose of exploring the mysterious well. [We] arrived at the cave [and] a rope ladder 100 feet in length with which we had provided ourselves before starting out, was lowered down the well, and [Ernest T.] Kirker [an editor of the *Manchester Independent*] headed the exploration.

"When about 50 feet from the top of the well, he called out to the party above to come down. We hastily descended to find our friend standing at the entrance of a narrow gallery leading out from the well. This gallery led back a considerable distance and got wider, debouching finally into a spacious chamber. The distance from the mouth of the well to the top of the gallery is 47 feet. From the roof of the gallery to the floor is 10 feet 6 inches. At its mouth it measures 5 feet 4 inches in width. The gallery is straight, 50 feet long, has a gradual descent, and where it enters the main chamber is 25 feet in width. The chamber [itself] is 225 feet long, 110 feet wide, and 24 feet high. The roof, floor and walls of both the gallery and chamber are smoothly finished.

"In the center of this chamber is a sarcophagus and mausoleum combined. The mausoleum measures at its base 55 by 35 feet. It is of simple though wonderful design, and carved out of the solid rock. Its base is paneled on all sides. These panels contain bas-reliefs are tablets full of written characters presumed to be memorials of the person or persons in whose honor the mausoleum is erected.

"The carving on the bas-reliefs is of the most delicate description and fully equal to the Grecian school of sculpture. The limits of a newspaper article [like this one here] will not suffice to fitly describe them. From the floor to the top of the base is six feet. The base is hollowed out at the four corners, and these excavations are covered with slabs of freestone, accurately fitted and so firmly cemented that a cold chisel struck with a heavy hammer made little or no impression on the cement. They are of uniform size, measuring five by twelve feet.

"In the center of the mausoleum rises a couch two feet five inches in height, twelve feet in length, and five feet in width. On the couch is extended the figure of a man. It is probably of life size, and measures nine feet four inches in length. The limbs are finely proportioned and disposed in an easy and graceful manner. The arms are folded across the breast, and the fingers clasp a bunch of leaves resembling the oak, reproduced with such a fidelity to nature that they look like petrifactions. Every vein and serration of the leaf is perfect. The figure is partially nude, a mantle or scarf crossing the breast and folding over the loins in graceful folds. The face is strong and robust in outline. The head is covered with a winged cap or helmet. At each corner of the couch is a vase, four feet five inches high, covered with beautifully carved flowers and leaves. Each vase is in shape something like an amphora, except that the bottom is flat and the handles affixed to the body of the vase. The neck is thirteen inches in length and tapers gradually and gracefully. The vases are of uniform size, although the carved designs are different. They measure in circumference four feet five inches.

"Suspended from the roof by delicate copper rods, directly over the head of the recumbent figure, is a copper lamp of unique design, elegantly crafted. At each corner of the mausoleum rises a carved pyramidal column, surmounted by caps that are unmistakably Doric. On two sides of the room are tombs of humbler design. They are side by side, of uniform size, and twenty in number, ten on a side. Like the mausoleum, they are carved out of the solid rock, and embellished with bas-reliefs. Their dimensions are as follows: length, twelve feet; width five feet; height, five feet. The tops are covered with slabs securely cemented. On the front of each is a raised scroll, covered with written characters similar to those on the mausoleum.

"On the wall of the room opposite the entrance are painted twenty-five faces, no doubt portraits of those whose bones lie in the tombs. They are faded and blurred, but still distinct enough to be deciphered. The colors used are red, yellow, black and white, and were evidently laid on with oil. The portraits are executed in a superior manner, and the anatomical proportion of the features is preserved to an exact degree.

"After our first astonishment over the[se] wonderful discoveries had in a measure subsided, we seized the tools and set to work to open one of the tombs. It was no easy task. Our chisels would not cut the cement which held the slab in place, and we were at last forced to batter the tomb to pieces. The walls were thin and a few blows of a heavy sledge hammer shattered the freestone to atoms. To our great surprise there lay before us, not a few handfuls of crumbling dust, but a splendidly preserved mummy, swathed in cloth, covered with a thick varnish, which emitted a pleasant aromatic odor not unlike balsam of fir. The mummy measured nine feet one inch in length, and the cloth in which it was wrapped, although of coarse texture, was skillfully woven.

"One of the party cut the wrappings from the face, but did it so clumsily that the head crumbled into dust. Portions of the hair remained sticking to the cloth and [this newspaper] correspondent brought some of it away with him. It is black, curly, and of fine texture. Besides the body of the giant, the tomb contained a spear-head, a hatchet, two lances, three mattocks, or hoes, a spade, a cup, two plates and a small urn, all of copper. I appropriated one of the lances and the cup as souvenirs. These wonderful people understood the secret of hardening copper, for an ordinary file will barely scratch the lance, and the edge of the cold chisel turns up like lead when struck against it. The cup is of softer metal, and beautifully engraved with trailing vines and wreaths.

"A square package at the head of the tomb, wrapped in the varnished cloth, was opened and found to contain a book of one hundred leaves of thin copper, fastened loosely at the top, and crowded with finely engraved characters similar to those already described. Lack of time and the total inefficiency of our tools prevented us from making further investigations. But when we ascended the well, we could plainly discern works of the sharp-cutting tools used in excavating the cave. In the first two chambers, and the last five [which had been described in the original article but omitted here], we had noticed many curious blocks of stone shaped like tables or benches, and presumed them to be of natural origin. Later examination [however] revealed the mark of chisel and pick, and these agents were undoubtedly used to fashion the entire cavern.

"In all probability the room was dry when the wonderful people who designed and built it were alive. The stalactites and stalagmites [in the cave] have formed since [human occupancy]. I measured one of the largest of the former. It was five feet six and one-half inches from base to apex. Allowing that it lengthened at the rate of one inch every fifty years, which a geological friend tells me is very rapid growth, it would have been 3,325 years reaching its present length. Conjecture alone can fix the date of the last occupancy of the cave. It must have been years before the stalactites began to form.

"I examined the mouth of the cave and discovered traces of a stairway which once led to the surface of the ground. Indeed, I found broken fragments of rock which, five or six thousand years ago, were undoubtedly parts of a broad staircase. There were also traces of a stairway which wound around the sides of the well, affording each entrance to the lower cavern. The upper cave must have been the cellar of a residence built above ground, and used for domestic purposes or as a place of retreat in time of danger. [The owner of the cave] intends to open all the tombs and the great mausoleum, arrange convenient means of entrance to the cave, and throw it open to the general public, charging a small price of admission to reimburse him[self]. Several parties have visited it since the discovery of the lower cavern, and all are impressed with the wonderful character discoveries. [The owner] is anxious to have a scientist examine the cave, and at his request a description of the discoveries, together with the engraved book, have been forwarded to the Smithsonian Institution [in Washington, D.C.]."

CHAPTER THREE

TOMBS AND TREASURES OF THE SANPETE VALLEY

The lost Jaredite tomb narrative to be presented here is genuine and true! There is nothing imaginative about it. The man who found it (and another treasure cave later on in the same valley) told the truth, though many professional archaeologists were of a contrary opinion. I ought to know because through the grace of God I became a reluctant participant in these very things myself when the original discoverer took me into his complete confidence. (The particulars behind how we met and why I too became involved are mentioned here and there in successive chapters.)

But to start things off right, let me quote the contents of a highly interesting article which appeared in the Wednesday, November 26th, 1975 edition of the Mormon-owned *Deseret News* (p. B-10). Living in nearby Manti at the time, I wasn't aware of this man or his unusual find, though it seems a lot of others were. My own strange immersion into these controversial affairs came a bit later and quite by accident as later text will show. However, the following basic information sets the stage for my own introduction of matters afterwards.

"John Brewer is a quiet man in his mid forties, about 5 foot 6 and frail. He has lived in Sanpete County [Utah] nearly all his life. Neighbors call him a 'collector' and say he has a knack for finding arrowheads. For a year, he has worked at the Moroni sewage [treatment] plant. Before that, Brewer held odd jobs to support his wife and five children, and he has been on public welfare at times.

"The amateur collector has been a thorn in the side of Dr. Ray Matheny, a BYU archaeologist, who feels he's 'wasted his time' exposing the man's works. Brewer specializes in finding inscribed tablets and plates. His first 'find' in November 1963 was a limestone tablet, but he has since reported finding plates of lead, copper, brass, and gold.

"In a report on Brewer's 1963, 1970 and 1972 'findings' of limestone tablets and lead plates, Dr. Matheny and an associate concluded that they 'are the meaningless work of a forger.' They base the[ir] statement on the following:

- The artifacts were found in areas of a type which were not usual archaeological sites.

- Inscriptions are sharp and clear indicating modern, sharp tools were used.

- Metal particles were found in the 1963 limestone tablets, 'suggesting that a soft steel tool such as a nail or pocket knife had been used to inscribe the stone.'

- Fresh cotton fibers and pine pitch covered the 1970 tablets. The pitch was not cracked or darkened with age as it should have been. 'Nor did it show evidence of exposure to moisture and soil for a long period of time.'

"A cryptologist, Dr. William S. Adams, attempted to decipher the inscriptions and, after careful examination, 'found so very few clusterings that form a language point of view that I am forced to conclude that instead of a meaningful script, the work was the haphazard scratchings of a forger.' Adams later visited the home of a Manti cattle raiser's widow for lunch and, upon opening a napkin which pictured some local brands, was dumfounded. 'There before my eyes were some of the signs I had so carefully copied from the Manti inscriptions.'

"Further investigation revealed that nearly one-fifth of the signs on the tablets apparently were inspired by registered Utah cattle brands. Since that time, Brewer has displayed—for school audiences and other gatherings—a collection of copper and brass plates, and tells of seven 'gold plates' he has secreted in a bank vault.

"His own story of the 'find':

"'I found the cave about 20 years ago, when I was 22. George Kelly, a Negro that lived in Manti, showed it to me after I gave him a couple bottles of wine. Inside the cave are big boxes with plates in them, two mummies (male and female), and a lot of gold stuff and figurines and stick-like things.'

"After the natural entrance to the cave fell in a few years later, Brewer said he dug his own 30-foot tunnel, which is now beset with natural booby-traps for anyone who might discover it. He feels it's a private place, his own little work area, and says he spends hours tinkering around in the cave, widening it, bringing plates out into the open. For years, there was a snag–the cave was on private property. But the 'old man' who refused to sell died, and his son then sold Brewer 10 acres, including the cave site, Brewer claims.

"Dr. Paul Cheesman of BYU's Religion Department has been trying to get Brewer to show him the cave, but Brewer has balked. 'Whenever I don't understand anything, I stall,' Brewer said, and his actions verify that. He has put Cheesman off for four years and, in fact, hasn't shown a single person the cave–including his wife and children.

"'Most people don't understand why I keep it secret,' he noted. The three reasons he gave this reporter were:

- 'I value my privacy highly.'
- 'Who gets the credit for finds like this? Always some professor working on his master's thesis, [but] never the guide that showed him the place.'
- 'I have three boys, and I don't have much money, I want to leave something for them.'

"Brewer maintains that at least three private collectors have 'offered me six and seven place figures' for the cave and its contents. 'I'm deep in debt, but so is everybody else. I won't sell. I don't expect anybody to believe me. And I'm not worried, either, because I know what I've got,' he said, with an emphasis on the 'I.'

"Matheny has had access to more recent plates exhibited by Brewer and says they are not genuine. [Brewer's] brass plates had the same 40-60 percentages of zinc to copper that is required by modern federal regulatory agencies. Besides, he said, 'zinc is difficult to process from ores and wasn't done so' until 1741. Matheny added that the inscriptions in the copper and brass plates had been made with modern chisel, and the plates were cut with scissors from the same metal sheet.

"'It is a clumsy attempt to perpetrate a fraudulent claim of antiquity,' Matheny stated. Dr. Jesse Jennings, U. of U. archaeologist, says the tablet which the U. of U. obtained from Brewer was a 'ridiculous hoax.'

"Meanwhile, Cheesman, has mixed feelings. 'They could be real,' he stated."

Almost two years before this negative article appeared in the LDS Church's official newspaper, quiet negotiations had already been going on with several prominent General Authorities of the Church in an effort to get them involved in this exciting find, somehow. Dr. Cheesman of BYU was the chief liaison handling such sensitive matters between John Brewer and Elders Mark E. Petersen and Howard W. Hunter of the Quorum of the Twelve Apostles and Elder Theodore M. Burton, then an Assistant to the Quorum of the Twelve (but later sustained to the First Quorum of the Seventy). After I got to know John Brewer pretty well, he told me that Elders Petersen and Hunter and Dr. Cheesman came to his home one afternoon and engaged themselves in a conversation with him concerning his unique finds. Cheesman did most of the talking, but the other two asked some questions occasionally. In response to one of them, Brewer identified the mummies and cave treasures as being of Jaredite origin; neither of the Brethren present seemed to mind this personal opinion.

But not only did I have Brewer's word on this very private meeting, I also had evidence provided to me by Dr. Cheesman himself when I visited him at a later date in his office at BYU. There he provided me with a photocopy of a letter dated April 10th, 1974, from Elder Petersen to himself asking for his assistance in bringing in fruition a possible visit between Brewer and Church authorities in Salt Lake City. The letter also indicated that the discovery of the ancient tomb in Manti had generated some discussion among the Quorum of the Twelve in their weekly temple meetings. (A reproduction of that same letter is included here.)

Furthermore, Cheesman related a second visit which he and Elders Petersen and Burton had with the man sometime in the Spring of 1976 (about a year before my own connection with Mr. Brewer happened). In that visit, he said, Brewer was pointedly asked by both of the Brethren, whether or not the things he had found were genuine. "Knowing who we are and whom we represent," Cheesman stated, quoting the words said by Elder Petersen, "are you willing to testify this day before your Heavenly Father, that these things are genuine and not—repeat not—of your own manufacture?"

According to Cheesman, Brewer blinked in disbelief at what he had just heard and gave them a disgusted look. Getting out of his chair, he reached into his shirt pocket and pulled out a half-used pack of

THE CHURCH OF JESUS CHRIST OF LATTER-DAY SAINTS

THE COUNCIL OF THE TWELVE

47 E. SOUTH TEMPLE STREET

SALT LAKE CITY, UTAH 84111

April 10, 1974

Dr. Paul R. Cheesman

Brigham Young University

Provo, Utah 84601

Dear Brother Cheesman:

I am returning herewith the slides that you so graciously loaned me. They certainly are very interesting. I think it is wonderful the work you are doing in this connection.

It is our hope that Brother Howard Hunter and I meet you before too long now and go down to Moroni on the other matter. Our brethren here are very interesting and it will not surprise me that we may get full control.

Yours Sincerely,

Mark E. Petersen

Copy of a letter sent to a former BYU professor of religion by a late Mormon Church apostle regarding the original Brewer treasure cave.

cigarettes and casually slipped one into his mouth. "I don't know what it takes to convince you fellows I'm telling the truth," he said. "I know what I found and I don't give a [expletive] who believes me or not. Now, if you gentlemen will excuse me, I'm going outside for a smoke." It was probably that laid back, care-free style and language punctuated with the dreaded "f" word that convinced the two slightly shocked General Authorities that this man had found something that was ancient enough, but they weren't quite prepared to go all the way in believing it was Jaredite or even related to one of the other Book of Mormon cultures. However, as Cheesman reported to me, "neither of the Brethren felt that the man had manufactured any of his finds" (as a number of scientists claimed he had).

While the particulars of how I connected up with John Brewer are given later in the book, it will suffice now to say that through the guiding influence of God, I visited an old family friend who taught religion at BYU and from him learned about this man, although he wasn't exactly sure of the town in which he resided. I made a stopover in Moroni, while driving back to our family home in Manti (where we then lived) and met Brewer for the first time. I listened to his story, knew in my heart it was true, and then parted ways with him. Since I hadn't pushed the issue of wanting to go to his cave, he became rather intrigued with this "unusual behavior"–everyone else seeming to have asked him for a personal tour sometime–and sought me out shortly after our first visit. Our friendship grew slowly and matured carefully before finally waxing strong in that kind of noble brotherhood to which all men should be bound.

During the period of time that elapsed for all of this to happen, Brewer periodically "teased and tested me" (as I like to call it) with regard to his mummies-and-treasure stash. I went along with this for a while, but finally informed him that my friendship with him wasn't based on secret caves or hidden records or anything else, just on knowing him as the person he was! He accepted this rationale and never again tried to "prove" my loyalty or integrity after that. But there soon came a time, one night at a late hour, when he showed up unannounced and was surprised to see that I was already dressed and ready to go, the Holy Spirit having impressed me beforehand of his coming and the purpose of it.

That particular night will always remain a historic moment in my life, for it was the night that I entered the world of the Book of Mormon in a very big and rather dramatic way. To put the matter in other terms: It was the night my testimony of this sacred record became granite-hardened and gold-enriched by the things I saw and touched and handled for myself. And though we would eventually part company in time over the mischief caused by someone with whom we were then both acquainted, my own witness of where this man took me and what he showed me, never once has changed. And even in spite of all the great heartache and terrible pain which our sudden and unhappy separation generated for me within, I still have always maintained that the two caves and their respective contents which Brewer had located on his own with great effort, are genuine and DO EXIST! Looking back now on those bittersweet times, I hold no grudges or, for that matter, no feelings one way or the other towards the man. His own life has come to ruin and the curse of God has followed in its wake with the death of his oldest son, Johnnie, not to mention his own mental deterioration. For over twenty years I have not cared to have any more association with the man, as I'm quite sure he has had similar feelings of equal intensity towards me. But well before his own miseries began and whatever alleged frauds he got himself entangled in later (long after our nasty separation), I still stand by the validity of those caves and their wonderful, ancient contents. At least in these two specific instances, Brewer's critics were all wrong and will someday appear as the educated fools they were when these and many other things are brought to light for the benefit of the world in general and the honest-in-heart in particular. Here now is the FULL STORY of one man's decision to take someone else with him, whom he trusted implicitly, into a realm of great archaeological mystery that had laid undisturbed for some two and a half millenniums.

We drove some distance towards a particular section of mountain situated to the east of the old U.S. Highway 89 that runs between the towns of Manti and Ephraim in Sanpete County, Utah. When we could go no further by vehicle, we parked and went by "shank express" the rest of the way. A clear, full moon shone that particular night, making it unnecessary to use the flashlights we brought along (though they did come in handy when wiggling through that dug tunnel that led straight into the cave).

My initial surprise came when he called an immediate halt a good ways up a mountain side and ordered me, then and there, to "strip down to your shorts and lay your folded clothes behind this bush." I distinctly remember turning my flashlight on and shining the beam directly in his face. He squinted and held up one arm to deflect the beam away. He asked me why I did that and I replied that I wanted to see if he was joking or not. He spoke with great soberness and inquired of me, "Does it look like I'm joking?" From that strict tone of voice I knew he meant business. I responded that I just wanted to make sure he hadn't gone weird on me or something to that effect. As I doffed everything but my boxers, he tendered an unsolicited explanation to put my mind at ease: "The tunnel is only so large and can easily accommodate someone my size even with my clothes on; but you're much bigger and will be doing good just to squeeze through wearing only the bare minimum." (As I sit at my word processor typing these lines, I peered down at my expanded chest, waist and hip girths, and realized that now, at the age of 53, I couldn't even make it into the tunnel entrance, let alone try crawling the rest of the way, without some very serious weight reduction done well in advance.)

He moved some brush aside and slid off to one side a wide flat stone that cleverly hid the tunnel entrance. "You go in first," he volunteered, "so that if you somehow get stuck, I can wiggle in behind and try to free you." I jokingly thanked him for his vote of confidence and reluctantly proceeded to crawl headfirst into the long, narrow black hole that lay before me. In doing so, I turned my flashlight on and pushed it ahead of me. The movement was slow and arduous; the cold damp earth around me gave my skin ten thousand goosebumps, not to mention a little chafing of the hide in a few of the tighter spots. I was thankful for never having been troubled with claustrophobia at any time in my life, otherwise I might have had some very serious anxiety attacks about then.

Brewer had instructed me that when I reached the end of this corridor, I was to carefully lower half of my body into the chamber and then slowly pull the rest of myself through without too much commotion. I soon discovered the reason for this: the floor inside was covered with several inches of ancient dust, fine as flour, and easily stirred with the slightest body motion. He soon joined me and we stood there in the dry deadness of the burial chamber, taking a thoughtful flashlight

24

The same inscribed stone slate (its broken fragments not mended with Super Glue) on display at the Joseph Smith Memorial Building (before its later extensive remodeling) on the campus of Brigham Young University in Provo, Ut. John Brewer loaned it to Dr. Paul Cheesman, who was a professor in the Department of Religious Education at the time, and who decided to put it on display much to the chagrin of university archaeologists but certainly with the encouragement and blessings of some Church General Authorities who were privy to Brewer's discoveries. The inscriptions are in an unknown language believed to be Jaredite in origin. (The Jaredite language remained unchanged at the Tower of Babel and, therefore, could by said to be the original pure language that Adam and Eve and their progeny spoke and wrote before the Flood.) This tablet remained on display for at least three years before finally being removed and stored elsewhere under lock-and-key.

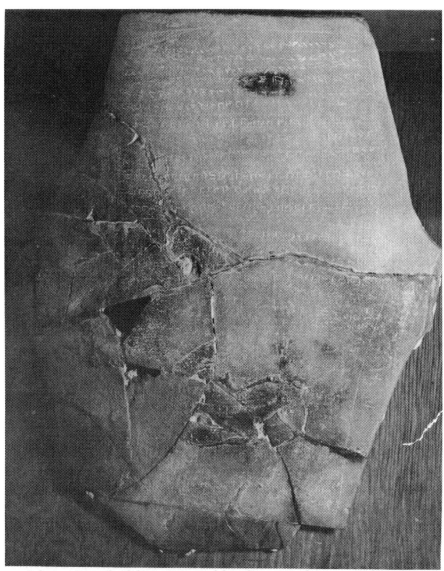

A large inscribed limestone tablet discovered in one of numerous caches scattered throughout Sanpete County, in southcentral Utah. A large map in the old cave enabled the finder to locate it. But in the eager haste of careless excavation, over half of it was broken into several fragmenets by a pick used in the digging process.

inventory of all that was housed therein.

The "cave" (as it has always been referred to by Brewer and others) was actually a stone chamber with several smaller anterooms flanking either side of it. The main room, however, contained numerous objects of incredibly fine workmanship and curious design. Against one wall there were a number of stone boxes wrapped tightly in juniper bark and smeared over with pitch pine to keep moisture out. The impression came to me that in many of these boxes were kept metal records containing the individual life histories and genealogies of many long-deceased Jaredites, who were once ruled over by the very large king and queen buried in huge stone sarcophagi located in one of the other, smaller rooms.

There were numerous weapons of war about the place, much as one would expect to find in the tomb of a great warrior or fighting king. Large, round metal shields made of a hardened bronze-copper alloy lay up against one wall. A number of massive swords, some sheathed and others unsheathed, both plain and ornately decorated, lay about the floor in no particular order. Some of the swords were manufactured out of iron, while at least two others seemed to be of steel. There was a big stone map setting against another wall, which Brewer had used over a long period of time to locate for himself a number of caches buried throughout the valley, as well as the location to a SECOND CAVE over by Wales, which he had never told anyone about until now.

That particular cave, which we eventually hiked up to a great distance sometime later on, was a naturally-formed affair of huge proportions. There were no buried mummies that we could tell of, but there certainly were greater numbers of stone boxes, both large and small, than what the old cave contained. There were also painted murals on some of the natural walls of the second cave that depicted varied scenes of important activities, such as hunting, traveling by chariot, and, most astonishing of all, sailing by boat somewhere! That cave appeared to belong to a later generation of Jaredites, who looked more Mayan in their features from the rock displays, than did the old mummies from the cave we were now in. (Those two mummified royalty appear on the cover of this book and look decidedly Mongolian, as I'm convinced most of the earlier Jaredites did. But time, climate, diet, and genetics itself have a way of remolding a people into something quite different than how their ancient ancestors may have appeared.)

One of the most singular objects I found in that old cave at a later date on a return visit with Brewer, was a curious piece of wrapped animal skin that when unrolled and carefully spread out, revealed the head of a gazelle-like creature with a single spiral horn coming out of the middle of its forehead. I was reminded of that piece of scripture in the Book of Ether (9:19), wherein it says: "And they also had horses, and asses, and there were elephants and CURELOMS and CUMOMS; all of which were useful unto man, and more especially the elephants and CURELOMS and CUMOMS. I don't know which of these strange names may have applied to this tanned hide before us, but there could be no denying the fact that the Jaredites once possessed unicorns! Here was proof for something that had always been considered a mythological creature by most scholars. The skin, in fact, had a soft sheen to it and, in some ways, reminded me of spun silk. I carefully rewrapped the skin and returned it to its original place, even though Brewer probably knew how badly I wanted to take it with me. But I always kept in view and never once lost sight of the fact that he was the host and I merely the invited guest; so I swallowed hard my occasional desires to remove such treasures as this and minded my "p's and q's" and behaved myself properly at all times!

In the event that the reader should be sympathizing with me about now over my own refusal to ask Brewer if I could have taken that unicorn skin with me from the premises, then consider something else that was an even bigger temptation and almost too hard to resist asking permission for. In one corner of the main chamber was a stuccoed, limestone box measuring 22 inches long by 15 inches wide and 12 inches high, and weighing close to a hundred pounds or the equivalent of a full bag of cement. It was unadorned of many of the raised pictures and inscriptions found on other boxes of similar size. There was no bark-and-pitch wrapping around it, and closer inspection revealed that the lid top had been carefully cut away for safer removal as well as to prevent possible breakage.

I shined my light in the direction of Brewer, who was off busying himself with some more records in another part of the chamber, and asked, "Did you open this box here?" He replied in the affirmative. I then inquired, "What's inside?"

"Open it for yourself and see," came the matter-of-fact response, so I took his suggestion, lifted the top off and set it aside. I then shined my light down inside and found what appeared to be several primitive coils of metal wire mounted or connected to two squat metallic post objects. Though I had a hunch what it was, I decided to ask rather than make a fool of myself: "What is it anyhow?"

Without breaking his own train of thought, Brewer kept busy with his own activity and flatly replied, "Oh, just some kind of ancient dry-cell battery, I suppose."

For me, at this moment, an adrenaline rush occurred that made it all but impossible to contain my excitement. I wanted to holler out exultingly and leap for joy at such an unlikely discovery as this; but better wisdom checked my runaway emotions. Still, I found it somewhat odd that a man like Brewer was attracted to "the stuff that glitters," while I, on the other hand, found immense happiness in the discoveries of the unicorn skin and this nearly 3,000-year-old primitive source of electrical energy. Brewer called me over to where he was and showed me gold plates, silver bars, and small objects encrusted with gems. I watched as he fondled them with much of the same affection that a miser would do his hoards of gold coins. The things that seemed to capture Brewer's interest at that moment, were to me so many cheap trinkets and baubles, which I wanted no part of. But the real sources of my excitement lay elsewhere in things of no apparent intrinsic value, but behind which still held inestimable worth in terms of animal existence and technological advancements.

At another time, both Johns returned to the old cave to inspect the mummies, the details of which are given in a later chapter of this book. Suffice it to say, their mummified skin and muscle tissue was intact enough so that with a mere press of the fingers, a slight resiliency was discerned. The Jaredite king or royal dignitary measured about 9 feet 2 or 4 inches tall and had rust-colored red hair, moustache and beard, while his lady friend who slept on a shelf beneath him in her own stone box, measured about 8 foot 8 or 10 inches in height and had streaks of gray in her dishwater blond hair.

With the passing of time, Brewer allowed and even suggested that I take some boxes from the old cave, with the intent in mind of having me examine their closed contents more carefully. I became satisfied with this and grateful for such privileges of trust. But I must confess, in all honesty, that the few times we returned to that first burial chamber over succeeding months, a portion of my heart was

Frontside of the same stone box. Observe closely that the scorpion image adorning this side of the box is slightly raised, as are other important images. The scorpion, it appears, was an ancient symbol denoting life and death. It apparently was in vogue before the flood as this author found an example of it carved into a half-buried rock in a field at Adam-ondi-Ahman, Missouri, at the site that Joseph Smith claimed was where Adam's huge altar stood in ancient times, upon which he routinely offered animal sacrifices.

Backside of stone box from the old Jaredite burial chamber near Manti, Ut. Note the extensive ornamental artwork depicting a life saga of some unidentified individual. It is thought that the enclosure to the left represents water travel in some kind of enclosed vessel with human and animal occupants and their necessary provender.

The top of the box lid depicts the image of a horse drawing a single-wheeled conveyance in which rides a human. This is proof that wheeled vehicles were known and used by ancient American cultures, contrary to the opinions of most archaeologists. (This same chariot, featured in another photo elsewhere in the text, is discussed in greater detail.)

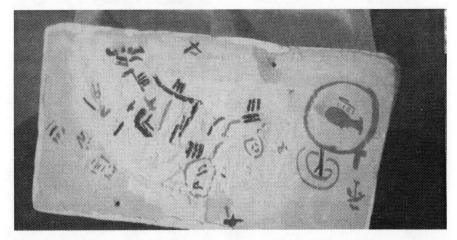

The inside bottom portion of the box lid. A little symbolic artwork was even apparent here in such an unlikely place. This stone box and lid were fairly typical of many larger ones found in the old cave. It was in such an unadorned white stuccoed stone box that I found evidence of ancient dry-cell batteries.

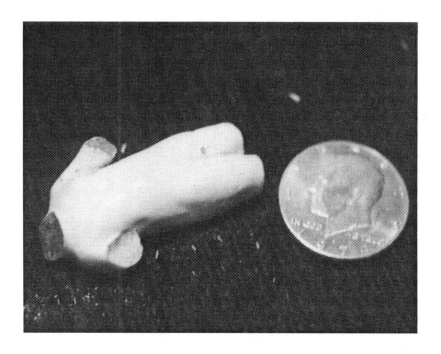

A porcelain figurine taken from the old Jaredite cave between Manti and Ephraim, Ut. Though the head and legs were gone, yet the remaining torso showed extraordinary ceramic skills. The intricate details given to buttock and rectal skin folds and opening on the backside of the figurine demonstrate an extraordinary craftsmanship for the Jaredites. This ancient figurine (presumably female) consisted of kaolin, quartz and feldspar that is typical for most porcelain objects.

always aching to remove the unicorn hide and dry-cell battery box from their rightful places to my own research facility for closer scrutiny. However, I had determined to have my conduct always be very circumspect when it came to any deals with John Brewer. And so, as far as I know, there these highly-prized twin objects set to this day in that dark and dismal mountain chamber, as silent evidence of animal myths-come-to-life and the unbelievable superiority of Jaredite technological skills. It is no wonder that with "treasures" such as these, the Jaredites will forever remain the single greatest civilization to have ever graced the earth since Noah and his sons!

CHAPTER FOUR

UPSTATE NEW YORK'S HILL CUMORAH, AN ANCIENT REPOSITORY

Of all the many hills or drumlins in upper New York State's Finger Lakes region, the most notable one is the Hill Cumorah (sometimes called in the past "Mormon Hill" on account of its long association with The Church of Jesus Christ of Latter-day Saints). Apostle Heber J. Grant gave us probably one of the best overviews of the ancient and modern history connected with this significant geographical site in an editorial which he wrote for The Latter-day Saints' Millenial Star (68:305-307) on May 17, 1906.

"The Hill Cumorah lies on the east side of the road between Manchester and the town of Palmyra, in Wayne County, New York, about four miles south of the latter place, and a scant two miles south of the old Smith homestead.

"Cumorah is the most distinct landmark in all that section of country. [It is] the highest hill and the most commanding in an extensive lain sloping northward filled with numerous hills. [They], in the main, have their greatest extend, like Cumorah, from north to south; and also, like Cumorah, are generally highest at the north end. West of this notable hill, the country south and east is broken and the numerous hills higher than on the west, yet such is the commanding height of Cumorah that the view is unobstructed for many miles. Some distance northward, hills are thickly clustered. Between them and Cumorah is located the town of Palmyra. Such is the Hill Cumorah and its surroundings.

"It is around THIS noted landmark that the last battles of the terrible Internecine War, which ended in the complete destruction of the Jaredite nation, were fought, early in the sixth century B.C. Here, also, according to the Book of Mormon, the Nephite nation was destroyed about the close of the fourth century A.D.

35

"But it is not as a monument which marks these ancient battle-fields that Cumorah takes on its chief interest. It will be known more especially to the present and future generations as the place where the Golden Plates of the Book of Mormon were discovered. During the night of the 21st of September, 1823, the angel Moroni [an ancient resurrected Nephite warrior-general and archivist] appeared to Joseph Smith at the home of his father. [He] made known to him the existence of this ancient record, and also the place where it was deposited."

Oliver Cowdery, an intimate associate of Joseph Smith's, who has often been referred to as the first scribe and second Elder of the Church by some Mormon historians and biographers, elaborated on this divine personage's unique appearance to the young man in a letter he wrote to W.W. Phelps, which was eventually published in the Latter-day Saints' Messenger & Advocate (1(5):79) in February, 1835:

"On the evening of the 21st of September, 1823, previous to retiring to rest, our brother's mind was unusually wrought up on the subject which had so long agitated his mind. His heart was drawn out in fervent prayer, and his whole soul was lost to everything of a temporal nature. All he desired was to be prepared in heart to commune with some kind of messenger who could communicate to him the desired information of his acceptance with God.

"In this situation hours passed unnumbered; it must have been eleven or twelve [o'clock], and perhaps later [in the night]. The noise and the bustle of the family, in retiring, had long since ceased. While continuing in prayer for a manifestation in some way that his sins were forgiven, endeavoring to exercise [his] faith in the scriptures [to this effect].

"Sudden[ly] a light like that of day, only of a purer and far more glorious appearance and brightness, burst into the room. Indeed, to use his own description, the first sight was as though the house was filled with consuming and unquenchable fire. This sudden appearance of a light so bright, as must naturally be expected, occasioned a shock or sensation, visible to the extremities of [his] body. It was, however, followed with a calmness and serenity of mind, and an overwhelming rapture of joy that surpassed understanding. And in a moment, a personage stood before him.

The Hill Cumorah with an upward view and the Angel Moroni monument in the distance.

Atop the Hill Cumorah looking down to the highway below in the distance.

"Notwithstanding the room was previously filled with light above the brightness of the sun, yet there seemed to be an additional glory surrounding or accompanying this personage. [It] shone with an increased degree of brilliancy, of which he was in the midst. And though his countenance was as light[ning], yet it was of a pleasing, innocent and glorious appearance. So much so, that every fear was banished from the heart, and nothing but calmness pervaded the soul.

"It is no easy task to describe the appearance of a messenger from the skies. The stature of this personage was a little above the common size of men in this age. His garment was perfectly white, and had the appearance of being without seam."

Resuming with Elder Grant's narrative about the particular treasure buried by itself on one side of the Hill Cumorah, we find that "while the angel was conversing with the Prophet about the plates, the vision of Joseph's mind was opened that he saw the place where the plates were deposited. And [he saw] that so clearly and distinctly that he knew the place when he visited it on the following day.

"The Nephite plates were found, according to Joseph Smith, 'On the west side of this hill, not far from the top, under a stone of considerable size.' The stone box in which the record was concealed was formed by laying the stones together in some kind of cement. In the bottom were laid two stones crosswise, and on these lay the plates, together with the 'interpreters,' or Urim and Thummim and breast plate. Following is the Prophet Joseph Smith's own description of the plates and the manner in which he translated them:

"'These records were engraved on plates which had the appearance of gold. Each plate was six inches wide and eight inches long, and not quite as thick as common tin. They were filled with engravings, in Egyptian characters, and bound together in a volume as the leaves of a book, with three rings running through the whole. The volume was something near six inches in thickness, a part of which was sealed. The characters on the unsealed part were small, and beautifully engraved. The whole book exhibited many marks of antiquity in its construction, and much skill in the art of engraving. With the record was found a curious instrument, which the ancients called 'Urim and Thummim,' and consisted of two transparent stones set in the rim of a bow fastened to a breast plate. Through the medium of the Urim and Thummim, I translated the record by the gift and power of God.'"

Just because he had been made aware of their location didn't necessarily guarantee that young Joseph would receive these Gold Plates on his first visit to the hill the next day. In fact, four years were to pass before he would be ready and responsible enough to take charge of this sacred record. In the interim, though, he met with Moroni once a year at Cumorah, "and there received instructions concerning the work of the Lord in the last days, how it was to be brought forth, established and governed," Grant wrote.

Prior to this remarkable visit from a divine being, Joseph Smith, by his own admission, had engaged in a certain amount of treasure-digging in company with other men, "but it was never a very profitable job to him, as he only got fourteen dollars a month for it" (see Elder's Journal, July 1838, p. 43, question #10). That there was a general public knowledge prevailing at the time of hidden treasures in and around the Hill Cumorah, may be evidenced from the following two short accounts.

Martin Harris, one of the original Three Witnesses to the Book of Mormon (the other two being Oliver Cowdery and David Whitmer), told some Utah Mormons in 1875: "I will tell you a wonderful thing that happened after Joseph had found the plates. Three of us took some tools to go to the hill [Cumorah] and hunt for some more boxes, or gold or something, and indeed we found a stone box. We got quite excited about it and dug quite carefully around it. We were ready to take it up, but behold, by some unseen power, it slipped back into the hill. We stood there and looked at it, and one of us took a crow bar and tried to drive it through the lit to hold it. But it glanced and broke one corner off the box" (see William E. Berrett and Alma P. Burton, Readings in LDS Church History from Original Manuscripts 1:63; SLC: Deseret Book Co., 1956).

Brigham Young pretty much verified the Harris incident with a true tale that Orrin Porter Rockwell, bodyguard to both Smith and Young, once shared with him. Speaking at a special stake conference held in Farmington, Utah on Sunday afternoon, June 17, 1877, he related this: "Orrin P. Rockwell is an eyewitness to some powers of removing the treasures of the earth. He was with certain parties that lived nearby where the plates were found that contain the records of the Book of Mormon. There were a great many treasures hid up by the Nephites. Porter was with them one night when there were treasures, and they could find them easy enough, but they could not obtain them.

"When [Porter] tells a thing he understands, he will tell it just as he knows it; he is a man that does not lie. He said that on this night, when they were engaged hunting for this old treasure, they dug around the end of a chest for some twenty inches. The chest was about three feet square. One man who was determined to have the contents of that chest took his pick and struck into the lid of it, and split through into the chest. The blow took off a piece of the lid, which a certain lady [Lucy Mack Smith, Joseph's mother] kept in her possession until she died. That chest of money went into the bank. Porter describes it so he says this is just as true as the heavens are" (see Journal of Discourses 19:37).

Joseph's first attempt at securing these Gold Plates was very unsuccessful; in fact, he met with bitter disappointment and a certain amount of physical pain when he repeatedly tried to grab them three times and couldn't. He had forgotten the angel Moroni's special injunction to him that such objects were very sacred and could never be used for any kind of self-aggrandizement. Because of the poverty in which his family then lived, the youthful teenager unwittingly gave Satan a chance to put the thought in his heart that such a treasure might be sold and the proceeds thereof be used to get his folks out of debt for good.

Oliver Cowdery, better than anyone else, knew intimately of these circumstances, for Joseph Smith related them in minute detail to him later on in his adult life. Oliver, in turn, put them in another letter to W.W. Phelps (a faithful church member at the time), who then published it for public consumption in the Latter-day Saints' Messenger & Advocate (2(1):195-198) in the October, 1835 edition. Oliver first begins his narrative with a description of the hole in which the stone box was buried, the box itself, and its ancient relics. Following this, he retraces Smith's first visit to the Hill Cumorah and his futile attempts to obtain this treasure for personal gain. His interactions with the angel conclude Cowdery's rehearsal of the facts.

"First, a hole of sufficient depth (how deep I know not) was dug. At the bottom of this was laid a stone of suitable size, the upper surface being smooth. At each edge was placed a large quantity of cement. Into this cement, at the four edges of this stone, were placed, erect, four others, their bottom edges resting in the cement at the outer edges of the first stone. The four last named, when placed erect, formed a box. The corners, or where the edges of the four came in contact, were also cemented so firmly that the moisture from without was prevented from entering.

"It is to be observed, also, that the inner surface, of the four erect, or side stones, was smooth. This box was sufficiently large to admit a breast plate, such as was used by the ancients to defend the chest from the arrows and weapons of their enemy. From the bottom of the box, or from the breast plate, arose three small pillars composed of the same description of cement used on the edges. Upon these three pillars was placed the record of the children of Joseph, and of a people [the Jaredites] who left the Tower [of Babel in central Iraq] far, far before the days of Joseph [of Egypt], or a sketch of both.

"I must not forget to say that this box, containing the record, was covered with another stone, the bottom surface being flat and the upper [part], crowning. But those three pillars were not so lengthy as to cause the plates and the crowning stone to come in contact [with each other]. When it was first visited by our brother [Joseph Smith, Jr.] in 1823, a part of the crowning stone was visible above the surface while the edges were concealed by the soil and grass. However deep this box might have ben placed by Moroni at first, the time had been sufficient to wear the earth so that it was easily discovered, when once [detected], and yet not enough to make a perceivable difference to the passer by.

"Two invisible powers were operating upon [Joseph's] mind during his walk from his residence to Cumorah. The one urging the certainty of wealth and ease in this life had so powerfully wrought upon him, that the great object so carefully and impressively named by the angel, had entirely gone from his recollection. [Now] only a fixed determination to obtain [this great treasure] urged him forward.

"After arriving at the repository [he made] a little exertion in removing the soil from the edges of the top of the box. A light pry brought to his natural vision its contents. No sooner did he behold this sacred treasure than his hopes were renewed, and he supposed his success certain. Without first attempting to take it from its long place of deposit, he thought, perhaps there might be something more equally as valuable. [Joseph reasoned that] to take only the plates might give others an opportunity of obtaining the remainder. [But if this] could

41

[be] secure[d] [also], would still add to his store of wealth. These, in short, were his reflections, without once thinking of the solemn instruction of the heavenly messenger, that all must be done with an express view of glorifying God.

"On attempting to take possession of the record, a shock was produced upon his system by an invisible power, which deprived him, in a measure, of his natural strength. He desisted for an instant, and then made another attempt, but was more sensibly shocked than before. What was the occasion of this he knew not – there was the pure unsullied record, as had been described. He had heard of the power of enchantment and a thousand like stories which held the hidden treasures of the earth, and supposed that physical exertion and personal strength was only necessary to enable him to yet obtain the object of his wish.

"He, therefore, made the third attempt with an increased exertion. [But] his strength failed him more than at either of the former times. Without premeditating he exclaimed, 'Why can I not obtain this book?' 'Because you have not kept the commandments of the Lord,' answered a voice within a seeming short distance. He looked and to his astonishment, there stood the angel [Moroni], who had previously given him the directions concerning this matter.

"In an instant, all the former instructions [and with them] the great intelligence concerning Israel and the last days, were brought to his mind. He thought of the time when his heart was fervently engaged in prayer to the Lord, when his spirit was contrite, and when his holy messenger from the skies unfolded the wonderful things connected with this record. He had come, to be sure, and found the word of the angel fulfilled concerning the reality of the record. But he [himself] had failed to remember the great end for which they had been kept. In consequence [of this he] could not have power to take them into his possession and bear them away [at that particular time].

"The heavenly messenger [then] said [to young Joseph]: 'You could not obtain this record. The commandment was strict. If ever these sacred things are obtained they must be [done] by prayer and faithfulness in obeying the Lord. They are not deposited here for the sake of accumulating gain and wealth for the glory of this world. They are sealed up by the prayer of faith, and because of the knowledge which they contain, they are of no worth among the children of men, only for their knowledge. On them is contained the fullness of the gospel of Jesus Christ, as it was given to his people on this land and it shall be brought forth by the power of God.

"'These things are sacred, and must be kept so, for the promise of the Lord concerning them must be fulfilled. No man can obtain them if his [own] heart is impure, because they contain that which is sacred. And besides, should they be entrusted in unholy hands, the knowledge could not come to the world because they cannot be interpreted by the learning of this generation. Consequently, they would be considered of no worth, only as precious metal. Therefore, remember that they are to be translated by the gift and power of God. By them will the Lord work a great and marvelous work.'"

Besides Oliver Cowdery, the other two special witnesses to the Book of Mormon—namely Martin Harris and David Whitmer—had some things to say themselves about the manner in which Joseph Smith obtained these plates from Moroni. Their combined statements give us a pretty good idea of the grave danger in which he had placed himself and his family upon receiving this sacred treasure. The *Deseret Evening News* for August 16, 1878 carried an interview of David Whitmer by a non-Mormon medical doctor—P. Wilhelm Poulson. Whitmer stated: "I saw the place where the plates were found. A great many did so and it awakened an excitement at the time, because the worst enemies of 'Mormonism' stirred up the confusion by telling about the plates which Joseph found, and the 'gold bible' which he was in possession of. So he was in constant danger of being robbed and killed."

Harris, on the other hand, had a great deal more to say about those early times when young Joseph often had to wrestle with devils both seen and unseen. In an exclusive interview he gave with *Tiffany's Monthly* (5(4):163-170), which appeared in the August 1859 edition, he made these revealing observations:

"Joseph did not dig for these plates. They were placed in this way: four stones were set up and covered with a flat stone, oval on the upper side and flat on the bottom. Beneath this was a little platform upon which the plates were laid; and the two stones [Urim and Thummim] were set in a bow of silver, by means of which the plates were translated, were found underneath the plates.

"These plates were seven inches wide by eight inches in length,

A stone box typical of the one that Moroni may have placed the Gold Plates in at Cumorah. This particular Hackmack stone box (named for the German archaeologist who discovered it) was found in Texcoco, Mexico. It is thought to have been made around 1500 A.D. The original was carved of basalt and may be seen at Museum Fur Volkerkunde, Berlin, Germany. (This replica was formerly exhibited at the Cumorah Visitors' Center until October, 1997.)

King Darius of Persia, in commemoration of the building of his great palace at Persepolis, placed metal tablets in stone boxes in the foundation. The engravings describe the boundaries of his kingdom in three of cuneiform: Persian, Babylonian and Elamite. Presumably written around 518-515 B.C. Originals on display at the Persian Musium of Antiquities in Teheran, Iran. (Formerly exhibited at Curorah Visitor's Center until October, 1997.)

and were of the thickness of plates of tin. And when piled one above the other, they were altogether about four inches thick. And they were put together on the back by three silver rings, so that they would open [up] like a book.

"The two stones set in a bow of silver were about two inches in diameter. [They were] perfectly round and about five-eighths of an inch thick at the center, but not so thick at the edges where they came into the bow. They were joined by a round bar of silver about three-eighths of an inch in diameter and about four inches long. [These along] with the two stones would make inches [in all].

"The stones were white, like polished marble, with a few gray streaks [in them]. I never dared to look into them by placing them in [a] hat, because Moses said that 'no man could see God and live.' And we could see anything we wished [simply] by looking into them. And I could not keep the desire to see God out of my mind. And beside[s], we had a command [from God] to let no man look into them, except by the command of God, lest he should 'look aught and perish.'

"These plates were usually kept in a cherry box made for that purpose, in the possession of Joseph and myself. The[se] plates were kept from the sight of the world. And no one, save Oliver Cowdery, myself, Joseph Smith, Jr. and David Whitmer, ever saw them. Before the Lord showed the plates to me, Joseph said I should see them. I asked him why he would break the commands of the Lord. He said, 'You have done so much I am afraid you will not believe unless you see them.' I replied, 'Joseph, I know all about it. The Lord has showed to me ten times more about it than you know [of].' I hefted [those] plates many times, and should think they weighed forty or fifty pounds.

"When Joseph had obtained the plates [from the angel], he communicated the fact to his father and mother. The plates remained concealed in [a] tree top [near the hill] until he got [a wooden] chest made [for them]. He then went after them and brought them home. While on his way home with the plates, he was met by what appeared to be a man, who demanded the plates, and struck him with a club on his side, which [left it] all black and blue. Joseph knocked the man down, and then ran for home and was much out of breath.

"When he arrived home, he handed the plates in at the window and they were received from him by his mother. They were then hidden under the hearth of his father's house. But the wall being partly

down, it was feared that certain ones, who were trying to get possession of the plates, would get under the house and dig them out. Joseph
then took them out and hid them under [an] old cooper's shop, by
taking up a board and digging in the ground and burying them. When
they were taken from there, they were put into an old Ontario glass
box. Old Mr. Beman [a neighbor] sawed off the ends, making the box
the right length to put them in. When they went in he said he heard
them jink, but he was not permitted to see them. He told me so.

"The money diggers claimed that they had as much right to the
plates as Joseph had, as they were in company together. They claimed
that Joseph had been [a] traitor, and had appropriated to himself that
which belong to [all] of them. For this reason Joseph was afraid of
them and continued concealing the plates. After they had been
concealed under the floor of the cooper's shop for a short time, Joseph
was warned to remove them. He said he was warned by [the] angel. He
took them out and hid them up in the chamber of the cooper's shop
among the flags. That night someone came, took up the floor and dug
up the earth, and would have found the plates had they not been
removed.

"These things had all occurred before I talked with Joseph
respecting the plates. But I had the account of it from Joseph, his wife,
brothers, sisters, [and] his father and mother. When Joseph came
home I did not wish him to know that I had been talking with them, so
I took him by the arm and led him away from the rest, and requested
him to tell me the story, which he did. [I found that his] family had
likewise told me the same thing[s].

"Joseph said the angel told him he must quit the company of
the money diggers. That there were wicked men among them. He must
have no more to do with them. [Also,] he must not lie, nor swear, nor
steal. He told him to go and look in the spectacles and he would show
him the man that would assist him. That he did so, and he saw myself,
Martin Harris, standing before him. That struck me with surprise. I
told him I wished him to be very careful about these things. He said the
angel told him that the plates must be translated, printed and sent
before the world. I said, 'Joseph you must not blame me for not taking
your word [on these matters]. If the Lord will show me that it is His
work, you can have all the money you want.'

47

A replica of the Gold Plates based on information given by Joseph Smith, Hyrum Smith, the Three Witnesses, and Elder Orson Pratt. The inscriptions on both front plates are facsimiles made from some of the Reformed Egyptian characters that were copied from the original Gold Plates themselves and taken by Martin Harris to New York City to Professors Charles Anthon and Samuel L. Mitchell for authentication. This was done by command of the Lord in order to give learned scholars a chance to either accept or reject such sacred things. They chose to reject them in fulfillment of ancient prophecy (see 2 Nephi 27:15-20 in the *Book of Mormon* and Isaiah 29:11-12 in the Old Testament).

"While at Mr. Smith's, I hefted [those] plates. I knew from the heft that they were [either] lead or gold. I knew that Joseph had not credit enough to buy so much lead [or gold]. I left Mr. Smith's about eleven o'clock [at night] and went home. I retired to my bedroom and prayed God to show me concerning these things. I covenanted that if it was His work and He would show me so, I would put forth my best ability to bring it before the world. He then showed me that it was His work and that it was designed to bring in the fullness of His gospel to the gentiles to fulfill His word, that the first shall be last and the last first. He showed this to me by the still small voice spoken in the soul. Then I was satisfied it was the Lord's work, and I was under a covenant to bring it forth.

"The excitement in the village [of Palmyra] upon the subject [of the Gold Plates] had become such that some had threatened to mob Joseph, and also to tar and feather him. They said he should never leave until he had shown the plates. It was unsafe for him to remain, so I determined that he must go to his father-in-law's in [Harmony] Pennsylvania. I advised Joseph that he must pay all his debts before starting [and] paid them for him. [I also] furnished him money for his journey. I advised him to take time enough to get ready, so that he might start a day or two in advance: for he would be mobbed if it was known when he started. We put the box of plates into a barrel about one-third full of beans and headed [sealed] it up. It was understood that they were to start on Monday; but they started on Saturday night and got through safe. This was [about] the last of October 1827 [or] it might have [even] been the first of November."

The rest of the story connected with Joseph's efforts to translate these Gold Plates into English with the assistance of various scribes, among them his wife Emma, Harris and Cowdery, as well as their being published in the final form of the Book of Mormon, are well known to most Latter-day saints. But the remarkable details of such can be found, for those interested enough to pursue the matter further, in *The Life of Joseph Smith, The Prophet* (Salt Lake City: *The Deseret News*, 1907; pp. 30-51) by Apostle George Q. Cannon.

While Joseph Smith ultimately escaped the clutches of a few evil-minded treasure hunters, it didn't stop them or others from prowling around the Hill Cumorah like so many ravenous wolves looking greedily for what they imagined to be other treasures of greater value buried somewhere beneath its surface. Edward Stevenson, another early Latter-day Saint who visited the Palmyra vicinity in 1871 and recorded his experiences of that memorable trip in *Reminiscences of Joseph, The Prophet and The Coming Forth of The Book of Mormon* (Salt Lake City: 1893; p. 13) offered the following in evidence of this:

"My loquacious guide showed me another and much deeper cavity made on the east side of the hill by [a group] named [the] Rochester Treasure Seekers, a company of prospectors. They said that science aided by mineral rods did not lie and that most assuredly there were rich treasures concealed in the hill, and they were determined to have them. But with all their science and laborious excavations, they failed to get a glimpse of the coveted treasures. [They] returned to their homes if not richer, at least it is to be hoped wiser men, for the only results of their efforts were the holes they left on the hillside.

"Notwithstanding this, there are strong and feasible reasons for believing that there is abundance of treasure hid up in Cumorah. But it is guarded by the hand of the Lord and none shall ever possess it until made known in the due time of the Lord. It was stated to me by David Whitmer in the year 1877 that Oliver Cowdery told him that the Prophet Joseph and himself had [gone inside the hill together and] had seen [a large] room and that it was filled with treasure. On a table therein were the breastplate and the sword of Laban, as well as the portion of Gold Plates not yet translated. And that these plates were bound by three small gold rings, and would also be translated, as was the first portion in the days of Joseph. When they are translated, much useful information will be brought to light. But till that day arrives, no Rochester adventurers shall ever see them or the [other] treasures, although science and mineral rods testify that they are there. At the proper time, when greed, selfishness and corruption shall cease to reign in the hearts of the people, [then shall] these vast hoards of hidden treasure be brought forth to be used for the cause of the kingdom of Jesus Christ."

David Whitmer, however, was much more specific as to when some of these other things from Cumorah's sacred repository would eventually be brought to light. In his interview with one P. W. Poulson, M.D., as published in the August 16, 1878 edition of the *Deseret Evening News*, it was reported as follows:

"The Book of Mormon is true, as true as any record can be. I saw the angel, and I saw the sword of Laban, and the breastplate, and the Urim and Thummim, and the plates, and the director [Liahona]. And the angel stood before us and turned the leaves [of those plates] one by one. [He did this, though] only [with] that part of the book which was not sealed. What there was sealed appeared as solid to my view as wood.

"About half of the book was sealed. Those leaves which were not sealed, about half of the first part of the book, were numerous. [But] there is yet to be given a translation about Jared's people's doings and of Nephi, and many other records and books, which all has to be done, when the time comes.

"[The plates are now] in a cave, where the angel has hidden them up till the time arrives when [those] which are sealed, shall be translated. God will yet raise up a mighty one, who shall do his work till it is finished and Jesus comes again.

"[The Temple of the New Jerusalem will be built in Independence, Missouri] right after the great tribulation is over. [By that I mean another] civil war more bloody and cruel than the [first] rebellion [itself]. It will be a [complete] smashing up of this nation [for good]. [At] about which time the second great work has to be done, a work like Joseph did, and the translation of the sealed plates, and [then] peace all over [again]. It was said to us that the second great work should commence when nearly all the witnesses to the first plates had passed away, so I may live and see these things take place." Unfortunately for him this was never to be realized in this life. But certainly the rest of what he said merits careful consideration and will very soon be fulfilled in the Lord's own good time.

Elder Heber C. Kimball, one of the original twelve apostles of the Church and first counselor in the First Presidency under President Brigham Young for many years, mentioned this about Cumorah's internal treasure contents in a meeting in the Bowery on Temple Square in downtown Salt Lake City on September 28, 1856:

"Joseph and others went into a cave in the hill Cumorah and saw more records than ten men could carry. There were books piled up on tables, book upon book. Those records this people will yet have, if they accept the Book of Mormon and observe its precepts, and keep the commandments" (see *Journal History of the Church* under the indicated date). And ten years later, "while at the Endowment House, [he] prophesied that when the final last struggle came to this nation it would be at the Hill Cumorah where both of the former Nations [Jaredite and Nephite] were destroyed" (see Wilford Woodruff's Journal 6:305 under the entry for December 17, 1866).

At the time that "the Prophet Joseph found the plates," noted the *Juvenile Instructor* (21(2):19) for January 15, 1886, "it is said a Mr. Randall Robinson owned the hill." But by the mid-1880s, "the east side and part of the west side [was] owned by Mr. Geo. Sampson [while] the balance of the west side [was] owned by Mr. Jeremiah Like." The Church eventually purchased this world-renowned New York hill in 1928 and erected a monument to the Angel Moroni on top of it in 1935. A visitors' center was later constructed at its base. And since 1937, the Church has staged the Cumorah Pageant at this historic site. Entitled "America's Witness for Christ," the epic depicts important events from Book of Mormon history. In July, 1988 a newer, more modern version of the pageant was presented; this total rewrite was commissioned by the First Presidency and completed by Mormon science-fiction writer Orson Scott Card. This author was present for the opening night gala event held on July 22nd. The extravaganza, though, lacked some of the reverent spirit which the older version seemed to have more of.

Interestingly enough, nothing was ever mentioned about the great hill's many other treasures, save for the Gold Plates themselves. Who among all of that vast crowd of some 7,200 on opening night were even aware of what once had been secreted below its majestic surface a while ago. Oliver Cowdery knew for he had been inside with Joseph at one time, and related his own experiences about this to Brigham Young some years afterwards. When he became Church President following Joseph Smith's cold-blooded murder at the hands of wicked men in Carthage, IL, he would make periodic reference to such things in public sermons.

From The Journal of Jesse Nethaniel Smith (Salt Lake City: Publishers Press, 1970; p. 217), we learn that sometime in February, 1874, President Young told a large assembly of Saints in Cedar City that some of the early brethren had been permitted by God to enter an apartment within the bowels of the hill itself. "He said there was great wealth in the room in sacred implements, vestments, arms, precious metals and precious stones, more than a six-mule team could draw."

Replica of the Gold Plates (from a former exhibit at the Hill Cumorah Visitors' Center that was removed in October, 1997).

Side view of the same artifact replica.

And again at a special conference held in Farmington, Utah on Sunday afternoon, June 17, 1877 (as reported in the Journal of Discourses 19:38), President Young repeated an expanded version of the same thing: "Oliver Cowdery went with the Prophet Joseph when he deposited these plates. The angel [had] instructed him to carry them back to the hill Cumorah, which he did. Oliver says that when Joseph and [he] went there, the hill opened, and they walked into a cave, in which there was a large and spacious room. He says he did not think at the time whether they had the light of the sun or artificial light; but that it was just as light as day. They laid the plates on a table; it was a large table that stood in the room. Under this table there was a pile of plates as much as two feet high. There were altogether in this room more plates than probably many wagon loads. They were piled up in the corners and along the walls.

"The first time they went there the sword of Laban [which Nephi used in the Book of Mormon to kill Laban with] hung upon the wall. But when they went again it had been taken down and laid upon the table across the Gold Plates; it was unsheathed. And on it was written these words: 'This sword will never be sheathed again until the kingdoms of this world become the kingdom of our God and His Christ.'

"I tell you this as coming not only from Oliver Cowdery, but others who were familiar with it, and who understood it just as well as we understand coming to this meeting. I relate this to you, and I want you to understand it. I take this liberty of referring to those things so that they will not be forgotten and lost. [Don] Carlos Smith [one of Joseph's brothers] was a young man of as much veracity as any young man we had, and he was a witness to these things. [Another brother] Samuel Smith saw some things [as did] Hyrum [who] saw a good many things. But Joseph was the[ir] leader."

When Joseph finally received the Gold Plates, the Urim and Thummim and the breastplate (the latter two objects made by the Brother of Jared several thousand years ago) on September 22nd, 1827 from the Angel Moroni, it was attended with some unusual heavenly fanfare that was witnessed elsewhere by Apostle Heber C. Kimball before he became affiliated with Mormonism.

"[He] related that on that eventful night he saw a white smoke arise on the eastern horizon, which formed itself, with a noise like that of a mighty wind, into a belt, as it uprose. [This] eventually form[ed] a bow across the heavens from the eastern to the western horizon.

"He further says: 'In this bow an army moved, commencing from the east and marching to the west; they continued marching until they reached the western horizon. They moved in platoons, and walked so close that the rear ranks trod in the steps of their file leaders, until the whole bow was literally crowded with soldiers. We could distinctly see the muskets, bayonets and knapsacks of the men, who wore caps and feathers like those used by the American soldiers in the last war with Britain.

"'[We] also saw their officers with their swords an equipage, and the clashing and jingling of their implements of war, and could discover the forms and features of the men. The most profound order existed throughout the entire army. When the foremost man stepped, every man stepped at the same time. I could hear the steps [myself]. When the front rank reached the western horizon, a battle ensued, as we could distinctly hear the report of arms and the rush.

"'Thus with signs upon earth and wonders in the heavens was the record of the mighty dead of this continent brought forth again by the power and wisdom of God.'" (See George Reynolds, The Story of The Book of Mormon (Salt Lake City: Joseph Hyrum Parry, Publisher, 1888; pp. 493-94).

CHAPTER FIVE

A PREPOSTEROUS NOTION—TWO HILL CUMORAH TREASURE CACHES?

This author has been to the Hill Cumorah approximately ten different times in his life. And each time that he has gone there, usually when the crowds are quite sparse, a solemn and dignified spirit has prevailed. It's almost as if he could sense with his soul the many sad and wonderful things which transpired around and inside of it in ancient and fairly recent times. Some years ago, during one of these several visits to the hill in mid-winter, he happened to share the solitude of that cold and forlorn day with four Catholic nuns, who happened to stop by for a quick visit.

These good sisters from some undisclosed convent and forgotten order became interested enough in the hill, after learning that the author was a Latter-day Saint himself, that they asked him to furnish them with a brief history of its existence. This he did in a very capable manner with the assistance of the Holy Ghost. He mentioned to them of the former contests of its interior which no one to date has officially excavated in a true archaeological sense (and probably never will for that matter). They marveled at what they heard, but were a tad bit curious as to why he had said "former contents."

This author explained to them his strong belief, conveyed to him by divine inspiration on a previous visit there, that Cumorah's more important contents, namely the vast amount of records stored there, had some time in the past (since Joseph's day) been transferred by angelic means to Utah, where the headquarters of the Lord's true Church now is. A couple of the sisters rolled their eyes around in mock disbelief upon hearing the words "the Lord's true Church," but all four seemed fascinated with the rest of the information. The author favored an unknown location somewhere in the wilderness of Southern Utah (below Bryce Canyon) for their likely current storage, instead of a place closer to Salt Lake City.

While much of what was said to them obviously seemed quite new and rather strange, yet to a person they all agreed that the hill radiated a special feeling of peace about it, which they had only felt at a few Catholic religious sites of importance that they had visited previously in different parts of the world. They graciously thanked this author for his kindness and we parted as friends. Though the outward coldness of the inclement weather had certainly chilled our bodies, yet the inward warmth from the friendships just kindled had kept our hearts and souls very much aglow with the love of Christ that we all share in different ways with one another.

Four 19th-century Church apostles, who visited the Hill Cumorah in pairs, themselves testified of its special spirit and unique place in the ancient history of the Western Hemisphere. Sometime in 1873, elders Brigham Young, Jr. and George Q. Cannon made a visit there and wrote up an account of the same which was published in *The Latter-day Saints' Millennial Star* (35(33):513-16) on Tuesday, August 19th, 1873.

"Undoubtedly great changes had occurred in the appearance of the surrounding country[side] since the days when Mormon and [his son] Moroni had trod the spot where we stood. Still we could readily understand, even now, how admirable a position this would be [from the hilltop] for a general to occupy in watching and directing the movements of armies and in scrutinizing the position of an enemy.

"Around Cumorah is yet a land of many waters, rivers and fountains [just] as Mormon said it was in his day. Our emotions on treading on this sacred hill were of the most peculiar character. They were indescribable. This was the hill Ramah of the Jaredites. In this vicinity, Coriantumr and Shiz, with the people whom they led, fought their last battle. For this great battle they were four years preparing, gathering the people together from all parts of the land, and arming men and women, and even children. The battle lasted eight days, and the result was the complete extermination of the Jaredite nation, none being left but the Prophet Ether and Coriantumr, who succeeded in slaying his mortal enemy Shiz. [Ether] and Coriantumr alone, of all that mighty race which had flourished upwards of fifteen hundred, were left. Who can imagine the feelings which he must have had on such an occasion?

Sign atop the Hill Cumorah giving a brief explanation of the unique history connected with this ancient repository.

One area on the hilltop that may conceal the hidden entrance to its interior treasure chamber into which Joseph Smith and Oliver Cowdery walked one time with Moroni evidently nearby to closely monitor their activities.

"From the summit of this hill, Mormon and his great son Moroni had also witnessed the gathering of hosts of the Nephites, and the dusky and myriad legions of their deadly enemies, the Lamanites. Around this hill they had marshaled their forces – their twenty-three divisions of ten thousand men each, commanded by the most skillful of their generals, all to be swept away except Moroni.

"It was here that [Mormon] hid the abridgement which he made of the records [of his people], and which is now known by his name [Book of Mormon]. And it was here, thirty-six years after this tremendous battle, that his son Moroni also hid his abridgement of the book of Ether, and the record which he had made from which we learn the fate of his father, Mormon, and his other companions.

"It was to this spot that about fourteen hundred years after these events, Joseph Smith, the Prophet, was led by Moroni in person, and here the records, engraved on plates, were committed to him for translation. Who could tread this ground and reflect upon these mighty events, and not be filled with indescribable emotion?"

Some five years after Young's and Cannon's trip, there followed a visit to the same hill by Elders Orson Pratt and Joseph F. Smith, a report of which was also carried in *The Latter-day Saints' Millennial Star* (40(49):787-89) Monday, December 9th, 1878 edition.

"In a beautiful little grove on this memorable hill, we bowed in humble and fervent prayer, rendering praise and thanksgiving to Almighty God for the treasures of knowledge and truth so long concealed beneath its surface. [This was] brought forth by the gift and power of God to us and the world in this dispensation. The spirit of prayer, of blessing and prophecy rested upon us so that we rejoiced exceedingly. After prayers we laid our hands upon and blessed each other, giving utterance as the Spirit dictated. We spent several hours looking over the hill, viewing the surrounding country, in meditation, prayer and thanksgiving. After which we drove to the little town of Manchester and returned to Palmyra, rejoicing and feeling that we had not spent our time in vain. We cut a few sticks, from near the summit of the hill which we brought with us as momentos of our visit."

That there has only been ONE Hill Cumorah ever (and not two as some have foolishly suggested) is supported by the reliable statements of numerous prophets and apostles of the Restored Church. On June 7, 1908 in a special Temple fast meeting, according to the diary of Ruth May Fox, "Pres. Jos. F. Smith said that he stood on the hill by Orson Pratt when he pointed out the site where General Moroni made his last stand against the Lamanites." Orson (as well as his brother Parley) knew better than most that THIS HILL in upstate New York (and not some other presumed pile of dirt in Central America) was the one, and the ONLY ONE, around which the final great Book of Mormon conflicts transpired. In the July 7th, 1866 edition of *The Latter-day Saints' Millennial Star* (28(27):417), Pratt wrote: "The hill Cumorah, with the surrounding vicinity, is distinguished as the great battlefield on which, and near which, two powerful nations were concentrated with all their forces. Men, women and children fought till hundreds of thousands on both sides were hewn down, and left to molder upon the ground."

Oliver Cowdery, who was Joseph Smith's faithful scribe during the translation of the Book of Mormon and in a much better position to know the REAL Cumorah from the spurious sites in Guatemala and Mexico suggested by others, gave the following correct data to W. W. Phelps in a letter published in the July, 1835 edition of the *Latter-day Saints' Messenger & Advocate* (1(10):158-59):

"By turning to the pages of the Book of Mormon you will read Mormon's account of the last great struggle of his people, as they were encamped round this hill Cumorah. In this valley fell the remaining strength and pride of a once powerful people, the Nephites.

"This hill, by the Jaredites, was [also] called Ramah: by it, or around it, pitched the [tents of] the famous army of Coriantumr. [He] was the last king of the Jaredites. The opposing army were to the west. And in this same valley and nearby, from day to day, did that mighty race spill their blood, in wrath, contending, as it were, brother against brother, and father against son.

"In this same spot, in full view from the top of this same hill, one may gaze with astonishment upon the ground which was twice covered with the dead and dying of our fellow men. Here may be seen where once sunk to naught the pride and strength of two mighty nations. Here may be contemplated, in solitude, scenes of misery and distress. Who can contemplate like scenes without sorrowing?

"In this vale lie commingled, in one mass ruin, the ashes of thousands. And in this vale was destined to consume the fair forms and vigorous systems of tens of thousands of the human race—blood mixed with blood, flesh with flesh, bones with bones, and dust with dust! They have long since turned to earth, to their mother dust, to await the [resurrection when they can finally] come forth, quickened and immortalized."

For those who may still prefer their erroneous "two Cumorahs" fable over the fact of the genuine New York Cumorah, there may be an inclination to dismiss Cowdery's views as merely one man's opinion. But this just isn't so. Elder Joseph Fielding Smith, one-time Church apostle and later its president, effectively squelched this line of reasoning in an article entitled, "Where Is The Hill Cumorah?" which appeared in the Church News section of the *Deseret News* for September 10, 1938 (pp. 1;6).

"The quibbler might say that this statement from Oliver Cowdery is merely the opinion of Oliver Cowdery and not the expression of the Prophet Joseph Smith. It should be remembered that these letters in which these statements are made were written at the Prophet's request and under his personal supervision. Surely, under these circumstances, he would not have permitted an error of this kind to creep into the record without correction.

"Later, during the Nauvoo period of the Church, and again under the direction of the Prophet Joseph Smith, these same letters by Oliver Cowdery, were republished in the *Times and Seasons*, without any thought of correction had this description of the Hill Cumorah been an error."

Unfortunately, history has often shown us that the proud and learned are more prone to perpetuate their own stupid ideas about certain "pet" theories they may have, instead of logically recognizing the truth of matters as set forth by those who've associated intimately with the prophets of God. Once again Elder Joseph Fielding Smith took up the pen in the February 27th, 1954 issue of the Church News (p. 2) to soundly denounce "this modernistic theory" of two Cumorahs, which he complained had done nothing but create "confusion and disturb[ance] in [the] faith in the Book of Mormon" of "some members of the Church."

"The Prophet Joseph Smith himself is on record, definitely declaring the present hill called Cumorah to be the exact hill spoken of in the Book of Mormon. Further, the fact that all of his associates from the beginning down have spoken of it as the identical hill where

Mormon and Moroni hid the records, must carry some weight. It is difficult for a reasonable person to believe that such men as Oliver Cowdery, Brigham Young, Parley P. Pratt, Orson Pratt, David Whitmer and many others, could speak frequently of the spot where the Prophet Joseph Smith obtained the plates, such as the Hill Cumorah, and not be corrected by the Prophet, if that were not the fact. That they did speak of this hill in the days of the Prophet in this definite manner is an established record of history."

One of Joseph's own brothers, the oft recalcitrant William Smith (who was once one of the original twelve apostles of the early Church) wrote this in a small booklet entitled *William Smith on Mormonism* (Lamoni, Iowa: Herald Steam Book & Job Office, 1883; p. 36) about the last great "terrible war" between the ancient Nephites and Lamanites: "This war commenced at the Isthmus of Darien [in Panama], and was more or less destructive to both nations. At length the Nephites were driven before their enemies north and north-east to a great distance. [While] gathering their whole nation together both men, women, and children, they encamped on and around about the hill Cumorah near where Palmyra, NY now stands; where the golden records were found, in the town of Manchester, about four miles on the road leading from Palmyra to the city of Canadagua." How else could William have been so geographically specific unless Joseph himself gave it to him first-hand?

Let a statement of Elder Mark E. Petersen of the Quorum of the Twelve Apostles, given in General Conference on Sunday afternoon April 5th, 1953 in the Tabernacle on Temple Square, forever put to rest the "two Cumorahs" silliness and limited Book of Mormon geography notion.

"I do not believe that we should accept every theory advance by men of science as though it were true. These men change their minds much too often for that. I do not believe we should give credence to the highly speculative theories about Book of Mormon geography. I do not believe that there were two Hill Cumorahs, one on Central America and the other one in New York, for the convenience of the Prophet Joseph Smith, so that the poor boy would not have to walk clear to Central America to get the gold plates. I do not believe we can be good Latter-day Saints and question the integrity of Joseph Smith" (see 143rd Annual Conference of the Church, April 4-6, 1953; pp. 83-84).

Elder Petersen's condemnation of such fanciful thinking came as divine inspiration during a Church General Conference. No one, not even the prophet then, President David O. McKay, felt inclined to set him "straight" afterwards or to disapprove any of these remarks. President Harold B. Lee had it right when he declared at the close of the 143rd Annual General Conference of the Church on April 8th, 1973: "If you want to know what the Lord has for this people at the present time, I would admonish you to get and read the discourses that have been delivered at this conference; for what these brethren have spoken by the power of the Holy Ghost is the mind of the Lord, the will of the Lord, the voice of the Lord, and the power of God unto salvation" (see *Conference Report*, April 1973, p. 176). Elder Petersen's severe rebuke of the "two Cumorahs" falsehood, backed up by President Lee's own declaration that ALL General Conference talks are inspired of God, is the wooden stake of truth driven through the heart of this theoretical vampire!

In conclusion, Cumorah's real treasure isn't the ancient artifacts that were long secreted beneath its surface, but rather the spirit of peace and goodwill generated therefrom. Long-time residents of the area may still hold a grudge against Joseph Smith, but everyone seems to love Cumorah. In The Autobiography of William L. Woolf (Salt Lake City: 1979; p. 143), this former patriarch of the Salt Lake University First Stake mentioned working with President Don B. Colton of the Eastern States Mission on the Hill Cumorah Pageant during 1936-38. "With respect to the nature of the pageant," he wrote, "I told Brother Colton of the extreme prejudice I had encountered in Palmyra against Joseph Smith himself. We decided that the pageant should not mention Joseph Smith's name or depict his life, but rather that it would deal with events and people written about in the Book of Mormon. We reasoned that the teachings of the book, being of high moral character, would soften prejudices against the translator of the records from which the Book of Mormon was translated, and could stimulate further curiosity concerning the book itself. The pageant was a great success in 1936, 1937, and 1938. The very cooperative New York Highway Patrol estimated the attendance at 70,000."

There was no pageant in 1939, though, on account of war breaking out in the European theater. Many Mormon young people volunteered their time and efforts in military service, the Red Cross, or some other way and church leaders deemed it prudent to not resume things at Cumorah until the war ended. Woolf wrote that a number of Palmyra businessmen, who had been before reluctant to lend support to the pageant, now were enthusiastically offering "to give us two hundred young people [from their town] as actors [who would be given explicit] instructions [to] not smoke or drink while on the [hill] grounds." He forwarded their collective letter to Church leaders in Salt Lake, "but those in charge did not consider it practical to proceed without our own people. I was, however, very much impressed by the inroads the pageant had made on Palmyra prejudice in three short years."

The spirit emanating from the Hill Cumorah is very real. One cannot imagine the degree of serenity and dignity it provides, no matter how active or vivid personal fantasy may be. And the irony of it all is that such calmness and respect for life comes from an ancient site around which so much intense hatred and tremendous bloodshed occurred. One who was deeply moved and visibly affected by the hill's unique aura was one of Palmyra's former mayors, Judge S. Nelson Sawyer. He spoke as an invited guest at the dedicatory services of the monument to the Angel Moroni, held on Sunday, July 21st, 1935 at the Hill Cumorah, and subsequently reported in the Church Section of the August 10th, 1935 edition of *The Deseret News* (pp. 1;8).

"All my life, nearly four score years, I have spent in this community [Palmyra]. I was born into an atmosphere of prejudice. I knew in my childhood and in my early youth, many, many people who lived here in 1830 and 1835, and so on down until one by one they were taken away. I knew many people who knew Joseph Smith and his family and his colleagues. I have heard those events discussed again and again, and I stand here before you and say frankly, with shame, that the prejudice which then was universal was instilled into the minds of the children, although they knew not why, and neither was it instilled in them knowingly; it simply was imbibed because it was as the air that surrounded them.

"Many years ago, when I was still a lad not entirely out of school, I met, one evening, two young gentlemen. Their names I know of, [having] passed from me years ago. I learned that they were Mormon missionaries; I learned that they were going somewhere on the errand of their faith. In the conversation that followed, I very

A view of the monument to the Angel Moroni
atop the Hill Cumorah

rudely made a slighting comment regarding the founder of your faith. (I have never had an opportunity to apologize, but I do it now freely.) [I did this] without any cause or reason whatever, but it was simply an outburst of that which I have heard all my life until then.

"These two young gentlemen, one of whom I particularly recall, flushed, but controlled themselves and then said to me: 'Mr. Sawyer, if you will go back to Jerusalem, they will there tell you the same thing concerning Jesus Christ whom you follow that you now tell me concerning Joseph Smith.' It was the most severe rebuke that I ever received, and, likewise, it was a just rebuke. [That young man] set my mind to thinking for the first time in my life, that like everything else, there might be two sides to even that question, although I had been taught otherwise."

Judge Sawyer apparently took what the one elder said very seriously and gave it considerable thought. A drive out to the nearby hill and meditatively pondering the matter further amid Cumorah's tranquil influence, evidently convinced him that Joseph Smith wasn't such a bad person after all. This "new slant" on things (as he appropriately called it) helped to allay his own long-inbred prejudice towards the Latter-day Saints and replace it with more of a humanitarian disposition. THIS is Cumorah's greatest gift to the honorable of the world who have graced its noble brow in times past and yet to come.

CHAPTER SIX

INTRODUCING THE GADIANTONS, AMERICA'S FIRST MAFIA

In the Journal of Abraham H. Cannon – he was a son of George Q. Cannon and a Mormon apostle of the late 19th century – under the Wednesday, November 26th, 1890 entries, may be found an amazing but true story concerning the founder of an ancient mafia-type society which periodically plagued inhabitants of the Western Hemisphere over several centuries.

"A rough spirit. Pres. Jos. F. Smith today told the following: Henry C. Rogers, counselor to Pres. Robson of the Maricopa Stake, became quite friendly with a Judge Hagan of Arizona, and the latter frequently invited Bro. Rogers to visit him. One evening the latter complied with the request, and at the judge's house a number of Gentiles were assembled and agreed to hold a spiritualistic seance. For some time Bro. Rogers prevented any manifestations [from occurring] by the exercise of his faith. But finally his curiosity was aroused to see the result of the spirits' works, and he drew up and placed his hands on the table with the others.

"Now the tapping of the spirits could be heard. Two taps indicated 'No,' and three taps 'Yes.' the Judge now began to ask who the spirit was – Geo. Washington, Joseph Smith, Brigham Young, and so on through a long list of noted persons. But the taps for 'No' were heard invariably. Finally, [it occurred to] Brother Rogers [to] suggest that he ask if it was Gadianton [the noted robber of the Book of Mormon fame].

"The Judge had no sooner done as requested than the [invisible] spirit [violently] seized him, and danced him around the room at an alarming rate. Chairs and tables were overturned, while the visitors, looking on in alarm and astonishment, moved out of the way of the afflicted medium. Finally, when thoroughly exhausted, he fell in a swoon on the floor.

"Bro. Rogers and Mrs. Hagan then began to rub him vigorously with liquor and cold water. And [Bro. Rogers] did some of his most earnest praying that his host might not die. After some time the Judge opened his eyes, and his first expression was, 'My God! I don't want anything more to do with Gadianton!' Bro. Rogers believed that around in Maricopa Stake [in Arizona] are located some of Gadianton's ancient strongholds. The ruins would sustain the theory."

Different Mormon scholars have defined the ancient Gadianton robbers in various ways. But probably the best "street description" of them comes from none other than Paul Rolly and Joann Jacobsen-Wells, authors of the popular gossip column "Rolly & Wells," featured in a tri-weekly basis in the *Salt Lake Tribune*. They (he is a disbelieving Gentile and she is a devout Mormon) defined the robbers this way in a September 8, 1999 column: "The Gadiantons were a band of thugs in the Book of Mormon who went around robbing, assaulting and murdering people." How something like this ended up in their column makes an interesting side-bar feature by itself: Utah Highway Patrol Trooper Paul Baily pulled over a good Mormon Relief Society sister for speeding near Kanab. Angry that she got caught breaking the law, she spitefully called the trooper "you Gadianton Robber." When news of this incident reached Paul Rolly, he had to ask around among some of his Mormon colleagues just who in the heck were the Gadiantons anyway before getting a satisfactory answer from one of them.

Anyone even remotely acquainted with the translated and published record from Cumorah, will invariably know that this Gadianton was one bad dude. But due to Oliver Cowdery's less-than-perfect handwriting, the typesetter at Grandin's Print Shop in Palmyra, NY couldn't distinguish very easily from his r and n, not to mention Cowdery's b and l. Thus, in the 1830 edition of the Book of Mormon (currently selling at a cool $65,000 on the electronic auction network known as eBay) Gadianton is once referred to in a positive sense as "the nobler" rather than in the more correct negative version of "the robber."

The Book of Mormon never informs us about Gadianton's physical features. We don't know if he was tall or short, thin or fat, young or old, dark or blond-haired, blue-eyed or brown-eyed, or single or married. But in the index to Volume 5 of George Reynolds' and Janne M. Sjodahl's *Commentary on the Book of Mormon* (Salt Lake City: Philip C. Reynolds, 1960; p. 356), there is this terse description: "Gadianton, expert in wickedness..." Probably out of everything that has been written about this nasty fellow, their rendering is the best synopsis of his entire character and career.

George Reynolds, who faithfully served as a General Authority of the Church (in the capacity of one of its First Seven Presidents of the Seventy), was ranked, according to his biographer, "among the five leading Book of Mormon scholars" in the Restored Church (the others being Orson Pratt, B.H. Roberts, Sidney B. Sperry, and Hugh Nibley). Bruce A. Van Orden in *Prisoner For Conscience's Sake* (Salt Lake City: Deseret Book Co., 1992; p. 204) wrote that Apostle Orson Pratt's "contributions directly influenced" Reynolds, who's work "in turn influenced" Roberts, Sperry, and Nibley. "His unique contributions to Book of Mormon scholarship," Van Orden stated, have widely influenced and affected many church members over the past 120 years; this includes "the first chronological dating system widely used today, [in all copies of the Book of Mormon] though rarely acknowledged." He also became "the first Book of Mormon teacher in the Church's educational system." Therefore, his work in this area must be given some serious credibility.

In *A Dictionary of the Book of Mormon* (Salt Lake City: Deseret Sunday School Union, 1910; p. 115-17), Elder Reynolds had this to say about Gadianton and his clandestine band of thugs:

"Gadianton [was] a Nephite apostate. [Around] 50 B.C. Gadianton organized his band, and bound its members together by the most horrible and blasphemous oaths and covenants, to stand by and protect each other in all their treasons, villainies and crimes. These oaths and secret compacts had not been searched out of the old records [of the Jaredites] by Gadianton. But that same being who had revealed them to Cain, the first murderer, had whispered them to him. Gadianton was a crafty, capable man, full of strategy and cunning; a flatterer, and expert in the use of many words.

"Of all the factions that separated themselves from the Nephites, none worked so much injury to the people as did the bands of the Gadianton robbers. The very fact of their organization shows the deplorable condition of Nephite society; while their continuance and growth proclaims yet more loudly and emphatically how debased the community had become.

"The Gadiantons were at first apparently, a band of robbers and murderers, bound together by the most horrible oaths of secrecy and satanic covenants, to aid and shield each other in whatever sins and iniquities they might commit.

"These covenants did not originate with Gadianton or any of his crew. They were as old as the days of Cain, into whose ear the Son of Perdition whispered these bloodthirsty and infernal suggestions. These same secret societies flourished among the Antediluvians, and had place with the Jaredites [another more ancient Book of Mormon civilization] and other peoples of antiquity. In the end they invariably wrought ruin and destruction wherever they found a foothold. To their abominations can be traced the fall and extinction of both the Jaredite and Nephite races.

"As time went on, the Gadiantons among the Nephites aspired to rule the republic. When, by their combinations, they could not carry their point at the elections, they would murder, or attempt to murder, any judge or other officer who was distasteful to them, and place a more acceptable man in his seat. So fell more than one of the Nephite chief judges. But they frequently had no need to do this, for as the people increased in iniquity they could easily carry the majority or the voice of the people with them. In this way several of their numbers were elected to the chief judgeship.

"After the time of the conversion of the Lamanites by Lehi and Nephi [30 B.C.], the Gadianton robbers took their place in the history of ancient America. The divisions then became the righteous Nephites and Lamanites on one side, and the Gadiantons on the other. And, strange as it may appear, these robber bands received greater encouragement and attained to greater power among the Nephites than among the Lamanites. But the fact is, that in that era the Lamanites were a growing race, while the Nephites were a decaying one. Many wars ensued between these two divisions, ending sometimes in the temporary suppression of the robbers, as in the year [17 B.C.]. But they soon reappeared, as they did five years after the instance here mentioned [12 B.C.].

"The most momentous of all these wars was the one that was waged during the earthly life of our Savior. It virtually commenced in the second year of His mortal existence, and continued with slight intermissions until the twenty-first. So powerful and arrogant had the robbers grown in that age that Giddianhi, their leader, in [16 A.D.], wrote an epistle to Lachoneus, the chief judge, calling upon the Nephites to submit themselves to the robbers and their ways; to accept their oaths and covenants; and in all things become like unto them."

It is worth inserting here the specific letter that this bold Nephite mafia boss wrote to the head governor of the land at the time. For the epistle gives us some insight into the brazen ways and highly intimidating nature of a very fearless, supremely cunning, and absolutely ruthless robber baron. It is found in 3 Nephi 3:2-10.

"Lachoneus, most noble and chief governor of the land. Behold, I write this epistle unto you. And do give unto you exceeding great praise because of your firmness, and also the firmness of your people, in maintaining that which ye suppose to be your right and liberty. Yea, ye do stand well, as if ye were supported by the hand of a god, in the defense of your liberty, and your property, and your country, or that which ye do call so.

"And it seemeth a pity unto me, most noble Lachoneus, that ye should be so foolish and vain as to suppose that ye can stand against so many brave men who are at my command, who do now at this time stand in their arms, and do await with great anxiety for the word–'Go down upon the Nephites and destroy them.'

"And I, knowing of their unconquerable spirit, having proved them in the field of battle, and knowing of their everlasting hatred towards you because of the many wrongs which ye have done unto them, therefore if they should come down against you they would visit you with utter destruction. Therefore, I have written this epistle, sealing it with mine own hand, feeling for your welfare, because of your firmness in that which ye believe to be right, and your noble spirit in the field of battle.

"Therefore, I write unto you, desiring that ye would yield up unto this my people, your cities, your lands, and your possessions, rather than that they should visit you with the sword and that destruction should come upon you. Or, in other words, yield yourselves up unto us, and unite with us and become acquainted with our secret works. And become our brethren that ye may be like unto us—not our slaves, but our brethren and partners of all our substance.

"And behold, I swear unto you, if ye will do this, with an oath, ye shall not be destroyed. But if ye will not do this, I swear unto you with an oath, that on the morrow month I will command that my armies shall come down against you, and they shall not stay their hand and shall spare not, but shall slay you, and shall let fall the sword upon you even until ye shall become extinct.

"And behold, I am Giddianhi. And I am the governor of this the secret society of Gadianton; which society and the works thereof I know to be good. And they are of ancient date and they have been handed down unto us. And I write this epistle unto you, Lachoneus. And I hope that ye will deliver up your lands and your possessions, without the shedding of blood. That this my people may recover their rights and government, who have dissented away from you because of your wickedness in retaining from them their rights of government. And except ye do this, I will avenge their wrongs. I am Giddianhi."

The sacred record mentions Lachoneus becoming "exceedingly astonished [at] the boldness" of the robber chief's exorbitant demands, absurd threats, and irrational vengeance. Wherefore, he issued a proclamation directing all Nephites still loyal to their central government, to vacate their homes in North and South America and gather together as one great host in the lands of Zarahemla and Bountiful, which Reynolds correctly identified in his Dictionary (p.87) as extending in the north to the Isthmus of Panama (where it was bordered by the land called Desolation) and southward to "the most northerly Nephite division of the South American continent" (or what is now present-day Columbia).

According to Reynold's account (p. 122), "the people obeyed, and in the trust of the Lord awaited the coming of the foe. In the latter end of [18 A.D.], the armies of the robbers were prepared for the war. They began to sally forth from their other strongholds, and to occupy and revel in the deserted homes and lands of the Nephites. But difficulties soon stared them in the face, the greatest of which was the want of food. As the Nephites had removed everything edible, the robbers' only source of supply was the game in the wilderness, which soon proved insufficient.

"Thus pressed, in the year [19 A.D.], Giddianhi gave command to his armies to attack the Nephites. It was in the sixth month of the year (September, we presume), that this command was carried out.

Terrible, we are told, was the appearance of the robber hosts. They wore a lamb skin, dyed in blood, about their loins; their heads were shaven, but covered with armor–headplates, as they were called. When the Nephites perceived them coming they bowed before the Lord in prayer.

"The robbers, seeing their action, counted it as a sign of fear, and set up a horrible shout and rushed upon them. The slaughter was terrible! Never had there been so much blood shed in a single fight since the day that Lehi's children first inhabited the land. At last the Nephites were victorious, and pursued their foes to the borders of the wilderness, giving [them] no quarter. Giddianhi himself fought with great courage, but being weary through his exertions, was overtaken in the retreat and slain. Zemnarihah succeeded him as commander of the robbers."

The final end (at least for awhile) of these plundering Viking-like hordes under their new leader, is given elsewhere in Reynolds' Dictionary (p. 341). "[In 21 A.D. Zemnarihah] came up on all sides in great force and laid siege to the people of Nephi. This system of warfare was, however, unsuccessful. The Nephites, who were gathered with their flocks, herds, provisions, etc. into one land, had laid up large stores of provisions, while the robbers had to subsist upon the game they could kill in the wilderness. The Nephites, therefore, adopted a policy of constantly harassing the robbers, making sorties by day and by night in expected places, and inflicting great loss upon the forces of Zemnarihah.

"The results of this policy grew so disastrous that the robbers ultimately changed their tactics and made an effort to reach the land northward. But being enfeebled by want of food, they were not able to act with sufficient rapidity. The Nephite general, Gidgiddoni being apprised of their interior, headed them off on the north and cut off their retreat to the south. Finding themselves hemmed in, the robbers capitulated, and those who did not do so were slain. Among the prisoners was Zemnarihah, whom the Nephites hung on the top of a tree until he was dead, after which the tree was felled to the earth. The robbers who had been captured were cast into prison, and by and by the word of God was preached to them. Those who repented and covenanted to murder and rob no more were liberated, while those who remained obdurate were punished according to their crimes."

Having successfully eradicated the robber bands from all over the land, both in North and South America alike by 22 A.D., the Nephites "did rejoice and cry again with one voice" of acclamation and praise unto the Most High for having preserved their nation. 3 Nephi 4:30-33 captures the deep gratitude which everyone then felt and gives us a sense of their profound appreciation to God for what He had just done.

"May the God of Abraham, and the God of Isaac, and the God of Jacob, protect this people in righteousness, so long as they shall call on the name of their God for protection. And it came to pass that they did break forth, all as one, in singing and praising their God for the great thing which he had done for them, in preserving them from falling into the hands of their enemies.

"Yea, they did cry: Hosanna to the Most High God. And they did cry: blessed be the name of the Lord God Almighty, the Most High God. And their hearts were swollen with joy, unto the gushing out of many tears, because of the great goodness of God in delivering them out of the hands of their enemies. And they knew it was because of their repentance and their humility that they had been delivered from an everlasting destruction."

To understand the oaths and covenants which bound the fraternal order of Gadianton brethren together, one must go back to an even earlier period in earth's long history. For, as Giddianhi observed in his infamous epistle to Lachoneus, "[Our] society and [its] works are of ancient date and have been handed down unto us." The Book of Mormon is very clear on this point: (Ether 8:15) "[These] oaths were given by them of old, who also sought power, which had been handed down even from Cain" and (Helaman 6:27;30) "That same being who did plot with Cain and his followers from that time forth. Behold, it is [Satan] who is the author of [these] works of darkness and doth hand down plots, and oaths, and covenants, and plans of awful wickedness, from generation to generation."

The book of Moses 5:29-31;49) in The Pearl of Great Price (one of the Four Standard Works of the LDS Church) explains something about the secret pacts which Cain and Lamech (a great-great-great grandson) made with the Evil One on separate occasions. "And Satan said unto Cain: Swear unto me by thy throat, and if thou tell it thou shalt die. And swear thy brethren by their heads, and by the living God, that they tell it not. For if they tell it, they shall surely die. And this that thy father [Adam] may not know it. And Satan swear unto Cain that he would do according to his commands. And all these things were done in secret. And Cain said: Truly I am Mahan, the master of this great secret, that I may murder and get gain. Wherefore Cain was called Mater Mahan, and he gloried in his wickedness. Lamech entered into a covenant with Satan, after the manner of Cain, wherein he [also] became [a] Master Mahan [or] master of that great secret which was administered unto Cain by Satan."

Irad, one of Cain's grandsons, becoming aware of this secret society "began to reveal it unto the sons of Adam," which made "Lamech angry," causing him to slay Irad, not "for the sake of getting" (as it was with Cain) but rather "he slew him for the oath's sake." The secret arrangements and understandings which Cain and Lamech had with Satan bore striking similarities with those oaths and covenants that Gadianton introduced to his renegade band, and which later successors like Giddianhi may have amplified. Now this next item may take a few readers by surprise, but is evidently grounded in some good research. It is proposed that Gadianton practiced a slightly altered form of antediluvian Freemasonry. In other words, a primitive version of today's masonry was known in Book of Mormon times.

But, more than that, Freemasonry was introduced to the world by Cain. Or, at least, so suggests two respected works on Masonry itself. Albert Gallatin Mackey's multi-volumed *History of Freemasonry* (New York: The Masonic History Co., 1906) makes frequent mention of this in its nine chapters. And G. Oliver's *Historical Landmarks of Freemasonry* (Cincinnati: J. Ernst, 1849; pp. 42-47) hints of the same in both text as well as extensive bottom footnotes.

Mackey draws on a number of old English Masonic manuscripts dating from the 14th century onward. The Halliwell MS. (Presumably 1390) and the Cooke MS. (Presumably 1490) both contain what is known in Masonic circles as Legend of the Craft (or simply Legend). This contains the traditional narrative of prehistoric Masonry. In his preface, Mackey freely acknowledges "that this traditionary story of Freemasonry which has been called the Legend" contains a great deal that is "apocryphal" in nature. But "these Masonic legends contain germs of historical [and] symbolic idea[s]" that, if "divested of certain evanescences or unauthenticated statements [may] almost always present in their simple form a true philosophic spirit" (pp. v-vi). All of the previously mentioned antiquated manuscripts begin their "traditional history of Masonry from the days of Lamech," who lived before the Flood (p. 15).

Oliver states that "the apostate race of Cain" stole from "the pious race of Seth" those "legitimate symbols" of pure Masonry and instead introduced a perverted version of the same among his descendants (p. 42). But because "the degeneracy of mankind became so great, and their perversions of pure antediluvian Masonry so grievous," it necessitated righteous Enoch (to differentiate from Cain's own wicked Enoch) hiding up the Grand Secrets of true Freemasonry on engraved marble "in the bowels of the earth." To make sure, though, that they would eventually be discovered in distant future sometime, "he built two pillars near the spot where they were concealed, with an inscription in hieroglyphics, importing that near it was a precious treasure which had been dedicated to God" (p. 45).

According to Joseph Smith and others, pre-Flood Freemasonry was practiced, not in the Old World, but right here in America. That is to say, Cain and Lamech and their Masonic brethren lived upon the North American continent. Wilford Woodruff's Journals (Midvale, UT: Signature Books, 1984) confirm this, for one thing:

[March 15, 1857] "President [Brigham] Young said Jackson County [Missouri] is the Garden of Eden. Joseph has declared this & I am as much bound to believe it as much as I am to believe Joseph is a prophet of God [5:33].

[March 30, 1873] "Preside[n]t Young said Joseph the Prophet told me that the Garden of Eden was in Jackson Co. Missouri. [And] when Adam was driven out of the Garden of Eden, he went about 40 miles to the place which we named Adam Ondi Ahman, & there built an alter of stone & offered sacrifice. That alter remains to this day. I saw it as Adam left it—as did many others. [And] through all the revolutions of the world, that alter has not been disturbed. Joseph also said that when the City of Enoch fled & was translated, it was where the Gulf of Mexico now is. It left that gulf a body of water (7:129).

[May 13, 1883] "A. O. Smoot told W. Woodruff that he & Alanson Ripley [were] surveying out [in] Adam Ondi Ahman about 22 miles north of Jackson County Missouri. They came across a stone wall in the midst of a dens[e] forest & underbrush. The wall was 30 feet long, 3 feet thick, and about 4 feet high above the ground and laid in mortar or cement. When Joseph Smith the Prophet visited the place and examined the wall, he said it was the remains of an alter built by Father Adam where he offered sacrifice after he was driven from the Garden of Eden which was located in Jackson County Missouri. The Prophet Joseph said it was upon this alter where Adam blessed his sons and posterity before his death. Let historians of the Church note this (8:172)."

Cain and his brethren became exceedingly wicked in their secret combinations. Their detestable order of Masonry was especially noted for its great cruelty and barbaric violence. Looting and pillaging were standard behavior for such depraved men. The ancient Jewish historian Flavius Josephus described it in these terms (excerpts of two different translations are used to convey a clearer meaning):

[Monsieur Arnaul D'Andilly's French translation of *The Works of Josephus* (London: Thomas Fabian, 1676: Book I, Chapt. 3, p.29)]: "After Cain (accompanied with his wife) had traveled through diverse regions, he made his abode at Nais. But he made not use of this chastisement for his better amendment, but rather became worse and worse; for he abandoned himself to all sensual pleasures, making it his sport to outrage those with whom he conversed, filling his house with riches gotten by rapine and violence. And gathering together other wicked and debauched men, he taught them to commit all sorts of crimes and impieties. He destroyed that simplicity which men before that time had used in their mutual societies, by the inventions of measures and weights; the ignorance whereof was the case that the life of man was estranged from deceit. He it was that first bounded the fields, and built the first city, and made a wall and a rampart, enforcing his followers to dwell therein. This city he named Enos, by the name of Enos his first begotten son."

[Sir Roger L'Estrange, Knight, English translation of *The Works of Flavius Josephus* (London: R. Ware, et al, 1755; Book I, Chapt. 3, p. 4)]: "Cain and his wife departed accordingly, and after a tedious travel through several countries, they took up at length at Nais, where they settled their abode. But so far was Cain from mending upon his affliction, that he went rather from bad to worse, abandoning himself to his lusts and all manner of outrage, without any regard to common justice. He enriched himself by rapine and violence, and made choice of the most profligate of monsters for his companions, instructing them in the very mystery of their own *profession* [italics added for emphasis]. He corrupted the simplicity and plain-dealing of former times, with a novel invention of weights and measures. And exchanged the innocence of the primitive generosity and candor for the new tricks of policy and craft. He was the first that invaded the common liberties of mankind, by bounds and enclosures. The first that built a city, fortified and peopled it, which city was called Enos, after the name of his eldest son."

When one reads at different times throughout the latter part of the Book of Mormon (especially in the Book of Helaman) about the deplorable conduct of the Gadianton robbers, it becomes evident that they were motivated, in part, by many of those departed spirits who once occupied mortal bodies and lived out their own depraved existences as cohorts of Cain and Lamech before the Flood. The Gadiantons own driven lusts for power, pleasure, and the wealth of others also helped spur them on in their many wicked deeds.

To live in such a society ruled by thugs and bandits in constant conspiracy with each other, would be extremely dangerous for anyone, whether they be antediluvian, Nephite, Lamanite, American or something else. To withdraw from a society filled with such avaricious and destructive elements would make a lot of sense for those seeking peace and safety from pillaging and plunder. For this reason did Governor Lachoneus order all decent, law-abiding citizens throughout his kingdom to remove themselves to a central gathering location somewhere between southeastern Panama and northwestern Columbia, where they could escape further Gadianton ravaging and instead find some solace in the strength of collective numbers.

For Noah, who lived at a much earlier period of time, it was no different. Only in his case, it involved not only the gathering of his own immediate family but also a large number of different animals into one Titanic-sized boat. According to Apostle Orson Pratt these "beasts of the field appeared to have more inspiration than the men and women of that age [and] began to come from the forests towards the ark" of their own free will. He designated them as "prophetic beasts...beasts that had revelation," good judgement and a great deal of common sense to save themselves from destruction in a watery grave (see

Journal of Discourses 21:174-175).

In The Pearl of Great Price (one of the Four Standard Works of the LDS Church), we read in Moses 8:20-22;28;30 some of the reasons why God finally decided to destroy all of the antediluvians save for Noah, his wife, their three sons and their wives. When Noah attempted to preach repentance to them, "they hearkened not unto his words." Instead they justified themselves by claiming to be "the sons of God," which entitled them to do as they pleased. For, after all, they argued, "Are we not eating and drinking, and marrying and giving in marriage? And [don't] our wives bear unto us children and the same [become] mighty men, which are like unto men of old, men of great renown[?]"

The extreme violence which then filled the earth was another thing which convinced God that something drastic had to be done soon. Violence was everywhere. The *Book of Jasher* (Salt Lake City: J. H. Parry & Co., 1887), an apocryphal work popular with many Latter-day Saints, described some of that violence this way (4:16-18): "They taught one another their evil practices and they continued sinning against the Lord. And every man made unto himself a god. And they robbed and plundered every man his neighbor as well as his relative. And they corrupted the earth. And their judges and rulers went to the daughters of men and took their wives by force from their husbands according to their choice."

We are informed in holy writ and by special revelation to the Prophet Joseph Smith that Noah's life was seriously threatened on several different occasions. Moses 8:18 states: "And in those days there were giants on the earth, and they sought Noah to take away his life; but the power of the Lord was upon him." And Joseph Smith told Dimick B. Huntington in Nauvoo one time, while he was waiting to get his boots repaired, "that Noah built the Ark in the Land where South Carolina is now; and that while he was building it and preaching, the wicked people mobbed and drove him [away] 4 times"—see the *Diary of Charles Lowell Walker* (Logan: Utah State University Press, 1980; II:730). Some non-Mormons were in agreement with Smith on at least this geographical point. Josiah Priest presented some pretty convincing evidence to suggest that Noah built his ark in America, "the country where Adam was [also] created" in his book, *American Antiquities and Discoveries In The West* (Albany, NY: Hoffman and White, 1833; p. 131).

D'Andilly's French translation of *The Works of Josephus* (Book I, Chapt. 2, p. 30) itemizes the extent of the wickedness initiated by Cain, the Master Mahan or Master Mason of this time, and his thoroughly vile fraternal organization: "The successors of Cain were most wicked, teaching and imitating one another's wickedness. The last of them proving always the worst, so that they were strangely inflamed to follow war and theft. And if perhaps some of them were more remiss than others in committing murders and outrages, yet were they rapacious enough to spoil and possess the goods and heritages of other men."

This absurd behavior certainly fits the mold and pattern for the Gadianton robbers a few millenniums later. Recall those parts of Giddianhi's epistle to Governor Lachoneus in which he spoke of both an "everlasting hatred" and an intense desire for Nephite "cities, lands, and possessions" felt on the part of his fierce comrades-in-arms towards all patriotic Nephites. A retired BYU professor of political science, who studied modern insurgency and counterinsurgency methods in China and Vietnam, wrote about some of Gadiantons' tacts in a past issue of *BYU Studies* (15(2):215-24, Winter 1975). Ray C. Hillam pointed out that these rebels carried out a "politics of terror" which heavily favored clandestine assassinations to liquidate their opponents. They operated in hiding, using special codes, secret passwords, unique hand grips, and other novel forms of signals that were virtually indiscernible in public.

As the Gadiantons grew in power, they became more sophisticated in their methods of pillaging and destruction. They maintained an "infrastructure with Mafia-like captains and soldiers," Hillam noted. Through this complex infrastructure they managed to "infiltrate both the Lamanite and Nephite societies" at once. They would carefully select their victims and targets before launching "guerrilla-type attacks against [both] the governments and people" of each nation. These rebels were intensely loyal to their leaders and were easily "whipped into the frenzy of battle" at a moment's notice. Recall Giddianhi's boastful claim to Lachoneus as proof of this: "...Many brave men who are at my command do now at this time stand in their arms, and do await with great anxiety for the word–'Go down upon the Nephites and destroy them.'"

Such societal infiltrations to scope things out before

conducting rapid 'attack-retreat' campaigns with animal-like cunning and cold-blood ruthlessness, fits a somewhat similar profile with methods used by the antediluvians. The only major difference between the two groups seems to have been that the Gadiantons almost never committed such terrible depredations on their own kind, whereas, everyone was fair game in the days of Cain and Lamech.

CHAPTER SEVEN

RECORDS OF CRIMINAL PERVERSION THAT SURVIVED THE FLOOD

Various apocryphal and pseudepigraphal works of ancient origin suggest that the antediluvians indulged themselves in a few extra favors of evil that were noticeably absent from the Gadiantons' own boasted acts of wickedness. The Book of Jasher (4:18) is quite specific on one of these: "And the sons of men in those days took from the cattle of the earth, the beasts of the field and the fowls of the air, and taught the mixture of animals of one species with the other, in order therewith to provoke the Lord. And God saw the whole earth and it was corrupt, for all flesh had corrupted its ways upon earth, all men and all animals." Here may be found evidence for the first clumsy attempts at genetic cross-breeding, but without the biological sophistication employed today.

Philo Judaueus of Alexandria, Egypt was a contemporary of the Apostle Paul, Jesus Christ, and the Jewish-turned-Roman historian Flavius Josephus. In his writing De Gigantibus (On the Giants), found in *The Works of Philo* (Peabody, MA: Hendrickson Publishers, 1993; p. 157), he hints at "the sons of earth" in Noah's day completely "removing their minds from contemplation" and instead "becoming deserters" to "adulterated" flesh. In other words, this scholar-philosopher of the Second Temple Period accused such men of "abandon[ing] the better rank which had been allotted to them as their own" (in terms of sexual engagement) and "desert[ing] to the worse rank, which was contrary to their original nature." This suggests rampant bestiality, among other things.

The Book of Jubilees in R. H. Charles' *The Apocrypha and Pseudepigrapha of The Old Testament* (London: Oxford University Press, 1976; 2:20, Chapt. 5, verses 2-3) presents the matter this way: "And lawlessness increased on the earth. And all flesh corrupted its

85

way, alike men and cattle and beasts and birds and everything that walks on the earth. All of them corrupted their ways and their orders. And they began to devour each other. And lawlessness increased on the earth and every imagination of the thoughts of all (was) thus evil continually."

For these three things – fornication with humans and animals, wanton violence, and gross injustice – were they destroyed. Another renowned translator of pseudepigraphal material, James H. Charlesworth, gave this version of Jubilees 7:23-24 in his own classic work *The Old Testament Pseudepigrapha* (Garden City, NY: Double & Co., Inc., 1985; 2:70) "And everyone sold himself in order that he might do injustice and pour out much blood. They sinned against beasts, and birds and everything which moves or walks upon the earth. And all the thoughts and desires of men were always contemplating vanity and evil."

The Sibylline Oracles, which are thought to have originated from the 5th and 4th centuries B.C. as ecstatic utterances from an old prophetess (presumably named Sibyl), illuminate the orderly manner in which only very selected animals were permitted to go into the ark: "The Most High appeared [unto Noah and said], 'Quickly go on board with your sons and wife and daughters-in-law. Call as many as I bid you to address, species of four-footed animals, and serpents and birds. I will subsequently put in the breasts of as many as I apportion life to go willingly.' Thus he spoke. [Noah] cried out loudly and then his spouse and sons and daughters-in-law entered the wooden house. But then the other creatures in turn, as many as God wished to save" (see Charlesworth 1:339, Chapt. 1, verses 200-210).

The Sibylline Oracles eloquently captured the full drama of the Great Deluge in these words: "[God] threw clouds together and hid the brightly gleaming disk. Having covered the moon, together with the stars, and the crown of heaven all around, he thundered loudly, a terror to mortals, sending out hurricanes. All the storm winds were gathered together and all the springs of waters were released as the great cataracts were opened from heaven. And from the recesses of the earth and the endless abyss, measureless waters appeared and the entire immense earth was covered. The wondrous house itself swam on the flood. Battered by many raging waves and swimming under the impact of the clouds, it surged terribly. The keel cut immense foam as the rushing waters were moved.

"But when God had deluged the entire world with rains, then Noah considered that he might look on the counsel of the immortal and see [this watery] Hades. He quickly opened the shutter beholding the great mass of limitless waters. Noah was struck with terror to see with his eyes only death on all sides, and he quivered greatly at heart. And then the air drew back a little, since it had labored many days drenching the whole world, and showed then the great vault of heaven at evening, as it were bloodied, greenish-yellow, and Noah barely [managed to] maintain his courage."

From assorted archaeological excavations, in various parts of Iraq in the 19th and 20th centuries, have come thousands of clay tablets and fragments that are now housed in the British Museum in London, England. Among this vast collection are tablets dating around 2000 B.C. that tell of the adventures of one Gilgamesh, the Sumerian equivalent of Noah. James B. Pritchard's *Ancient Near Eastern Texts Relating to the Old Testament* (Princeton, NJ: Princeton University Press, 1969; p. 94) contains portions of "The Deluge Epic" involving him. This Noah figure describes what happened next when the winds abated, the water subsided and things settled down in general.

"The sea grew quiet, the tempest was still, the flood ceased. I looked at the weather: stillness had set in, and all of mankind had returned to clay. The landscape was as level as a flat roof. I opened a hatch, and light fell upon my face. Bowing low, I saw and wept tears running down off my face. I looked about for coast lines in the expanse of the sea. There emerged a mountain-region. On mount Nisir [Ararat] the ship came to halt and held fast, allowing no motion." Gilgamesh/Noah sent forth a dove, a swallow, and a raven before determining that the ark's numerous occupants could safely set foot on dry land again.

Now some people might consider such horrific destruction of life, limb, and property to have been cruel and unkind behavior for a normally benevolent and loving god. But there was plenty of justification for it, as Elder B. H. Roberts pointed out at the Weber Stake Conference in the Ogden Tabernacle on July 16th, 1893 (see *Millennial Star* 55:701): "God knew that if that generation of men were permitted to continue propagating their species, the result would be that a curse and not a blessing would be brought upon His children who lived with

Him in heaven [at the time]. In justice, then, to the untold millions of spirits that were to come to the earth, the Lord destroyed that generation of men that lived in the days of Noah. I see in that an act of mercy rather than cruelty. The people in the days of Noah were cut off from the earth that their wickedness might not be perpetuated in their children. And a more righteous branch of the human family was preserved, that the spirits that had to tabernacle in the flesh might have a better parentage than the wicked antediluvians. And consequently [have] a better prospect of successfully accomplishing their mission in this probation than they would by coming through a wicked parentage."

According to the history science journal *Antiquity* (54:34-36) for March, 1980, the ark presently rests "in northeastern Turkey [in an] extinct volcanic complex [called] Aghri Daghi." Mount Ararat "actually consists of two neighboring peaks," a higher (16,950 ft.) and a lower (12,880 ft.) one. "On the northwest side of the major [or bigger] peak is a series of glaciers flowing from a permanent ice field." This is where the ark is believed to still be preserved over four millenniums later. Ancient wood fragments obtained at lower levels by a few individuals seem to show that the ark was built out of oak and oleander; both woods are strongly resistant to rot and can last for many centuries.

Noah brought with him some of the ancient records that had been kept in pre-Flood days. The Book of Mormon informs us of that much (Ether 8:9) when the Jaredite temptress, known only as 'the daughter of Jared' reminded her father of them in order to cheer him up: "Hath my father not read the record which our fathers brought across the great deep? Behold, is there not an account concerning them of old, that they by their secret plans did obtain kingdoms and great glory?" In his original footnotes in those copies of the Book of Mormon printed before 1920, Apostle Orson Pratt stated at the bottom of the page, on which Ether 8 opens, that "the record" was merely "a copy of the scriptures from the creation to the Tower of Babel." And, furthermore, that those "secret plans" contained therein "originated in the days of Cain." Here then we find a direct source for Gadianton of a much later time period. Recall again, if you will, what the robber chieftain Giddianhi told the Nephite governor Lachoneus in his document sent to the latter: "[We are a] secret society; which society and the works thereof are of ancient date and have been handed down unto us."

But besides ancient scriptures, there may have been "other records" kept by dark sources which made their way, though in carefully concealed fashion, across the flood in the ark. These were brought over by Ham and his wife. Their genealogies, to say the least, are certainly quite interesting to our story in general. A careful reading of Moses 8:12 in The Pearl of Great Price definitely shows that while Japheth and Shem were blood brothers and shared the same mother, Ham did not, which suggests he may have been adopted into the family of Noah or else born from a separate mother. Also, he "had married a daughter of Cain, and by him the curse [brought on Cain] was carried through the flood." Ham had a despicable nature about himself. The Journal of Abraham H. Cannon informs us, under the entry of Tuesday, March 29th, 1892, that Ham's real sin "consisted in trying to castrate his father, Noah" when he laid upon his bed naked and accidentally drunk, as well as for trying to "kill his brothers, Shem and Japheth, so that he [could] become the head of the nations of the earth." Wilford Woodruff's Journal (2:137) under the entry date of Sunday, November 7th, 1841 mentions that Ham was also cursed "for laughing" at his father while the man was in his drunken stupor and passed out "in an unseemly position" on his bed. (Both reference statements are attributed to the Prophet Joseph Smith.)

According to the apocryphal Book of Jasher (7:26-29) Ham was a thief and stole sacred clothing and other valuable relics of religious significance from his father, Noah. These he hid away from his brothers Japheth and Shem and eventually passed them on to his first-born son Cush, who "also concealed them from his sons and brothers," and then later on made presents of them to his son Nimrod. Among these stolen items must have been some of the books or records kept by Cain and Lamech of their fraternal Masonic order and its numerous evil activities. A pseudepigraphal work written around the time of Jesus and with apparent access to information from more ancient sources, is Pseudo-Philo. In its retelling of pre-Flood times, it "stands close in form to Jubilees, the *Qumran Genesis Apocryphon*, and *Josephus' Antiquities [of The Jews]*," according to James H. Charlesworth (2:229;302;305). Pseudo-Philo recounts that "Cain was fifteen years old" and married to Themech his wife when he "killed

Abel his brother." (The Prophet Joseph Smith pinpointed the location where earth's first murder took place: It happened in Far West, Missouri, quite near a dedicated temple site.) Cain also started keeping a written account about this time of his secret society and their evil doings.

It is not unreasonable at all to consider that the daughter of Cain who married Ham didn't somehow smuggle her father's records aboard the ark with the rest of their needful paraphernalia. They were then passed on to Cush and from there later to Nimrod. When Jared (after whom the Book of Mormon Jaredites were named) and his brother labored on the massive public works project in the Plains of Shinar, known as the Tower of Babel, they apparently acquired Cain's record with some of his dark descendants, who came with the brothers and their large entourage when they left that place and eventually migrated across the Pacific Ocean in eight barges to the Western Hemisphere, landing just below Baja, California somewhere.

CHAPTER EIGHT

CURSED TREASURE SITES OF THE EVIL ONES

Following the devastating genocidal wars among the Jaredites that left them pretty well extinct as a civilization (except for a few stragglers here and there), the Nephites and Lamanites in South America and the Mulekites in Central America commenced growing as separate nations. Over the course of several centuries, various secret combination societies sprung up among the Nephites and Lamanites – Mulekites (then known as the people of Zarahemla) had by then become successfully integrated with the Nephites. These small, often short-lived rebel groups were the actual forerunners to Gadianton and his tribe. Until he came along, the others were nothing more than two-bit hoodlums and religious crackpots. But when this particular "expert in wickedness" stepped into the picture, things really changed.

Gadianton brought a sophistication and style never before seen in a Mafia-like organization. He had the glib tongue of an orator, the persuasive abilities of a criminal lawyer, the marketing genius of an advertising executive, the positive enthusiasm of a public relations person, and the drive and energy of a competing athlete. He had just enough religious trappings about himself to appear somewhat devout in the eyes of others. And true to his chameleon character, he was capable of quickly changing himself into becoming whatever others wished for him to be. He was, in fact, the consummate Nephite politician extraordinaire.

With time and some patience on his side, this highly resourceful individual sought to expand the power and influence of his group over much of the Nephite nation. At various times, though, when he and his associates were close to getting caught by the Nephite military, they escaped by moving further northward until they eventually penetrated the isolated wilderness waste regions of western Nevada, northern Arizona, and pretty much all of Utah, especially the southern and southwestern regions of the state, according to Church

President Brigham Young (see *The Contributor* 15:323).

The Book of Mormon (4 Nephi 1:46) correctly informs us that by 320 A.D. both the Nephites and Lamanites had become so prosperous that "gold and silver did they lay up in store in abundance," while at the same time "the robbers of Gadianton did spread over all the face of the land." Exceedingly prosperous times brought out the best criminality in these bandits, as they went on their many marauding forays and bringing back to their high mountain stashes unbelievable accumulations of plundered wealth.

Brigham Young was especially sensitive to the invisible lingering presence of so many of these disembodied spirits and at various times in his leadership career as prophet, seer, and revelator to the Latter-day Saints, could identify different places in Utah where many of them liked to hang out. In a small biographical tract published in May, 1943 and entitled James H. Gardner, Historical Pamphlet, mention is made of grounds in Mill Creek Canyon and Big Cottonwood Canyon just east of Salt Lake City that were formerly sacred to the Gadiantons.

"In the 1850's, in Mill Creek Canyon there was a saw mill owned by Alexander. While using his tools, files, axes, etc., he would lose them. He would put a file down, and turn and it was gone. As long as the tools were in his hands they were safe, but if he put them down they were gone. [This continued on for some time.] Alexander was advised to go and see B[righam] Young and be advised on what to do.

"He was told that he was trespassing on property belonging to the Gadianton Robbers, a spot where they held their secret gatherings. [He was] told to get some of the [priesthood] brethren to join him in a prayer circle. Dressed in their holy [temple] robes, this was done. B. Young told them to move the mill to other parts. When the slab pile in the creek was hauled away, which was about twenty feet deep, behold, there were axes, chains and everything that was lost. Thus ended the story of the Alexander saw mill.

"A few years later [the] Maxfield Brothers started to build a saw mill in Big Cottonwood Canyon and they had the same trouble. They asked B. Young to go up to the mill with them, showing him the location and what had happened. He told them also that the mill was on a sacred spot to the Gadianton Robbers and advised them to move to the other end of the flat, about 200 yards, which they did and had no more trouble [after that]."

During a sermon given in the Old Tabernacle on Temple Block in Salt Lake City on January 20th, 1861, Young stated: "There are scores of evil spirits here – spirits of the old Gadianton Robbers, some of whom inhabited these mountains, and used to go into the South and afflict the Nephites. There are millions of those spirits in the mountains, and they are ready to make us covetous, if they can. They are ready to lead astray every man and woman that wishes to be a Latter-day Saint. This may seem strange to some of you, but you will see them." And again in another sermon given in the same place just six years later on December 29th, 1867, he made this significant statement: "The spirits of the ancient Gadiantons are around us. You may see battlefield after battlefield, scattered over this American continent, where the wicked have slain the wicked. Their spirits are watching us continually for an opportunity to influence us to do evil, or to make us decline in the performance of our duties." (See *Journal of Discourses* 8:344 and 12:128 respectively.)

But he really scared the daylights out of some faithful Saints in St. George on Sunday, May 14th, 1876 when he came there to dedicate the new Tabernacle building. His son Brigham Young, Jr. offered the dedicatory prayer. Four choirs were present, composed of faithful church members from the nearby communities of Cedar City, Kanab, Santa Clara and, of course, St. George itself.

The customary "Hosanna Shout" was enthusiastically given three times by over a thousand people tightly crowded into the new edifice. The large congregation stood and in unison shouted the words "Hosanna, Hosanna, Hosanna to God and the Lamb, Amen, Amen, and Amen," while at the same time rhythmically waving white handkerchiefs with uplifted hands.

Following addresses by James G. Bleak and by one of Brigham's daughters, Susa Young Gates, Brigham Young slowly got up out of his chair and with the aid of a walking cane hobbled to the pulpit. An enlarged prostate was giving him urinary problems again, which had resulted in an aggressive flaring up of rheumatism. Yet his mind was still sharp and voice vigorous enough to let his message roll across the hall in booming fashion. Mary Catherine Jolley Blazzard was one of those in attendance that historic day with her husband James. She recounted highlights of the great Mormon leader's stirring sermon, which appeared in a printed family history some years ago, *The Jolly Family Book* (Provo: BYU Press, 1966; p. 429):

"Brigham Young reminded the settlers in detail of the hardship they had endured in the new country. He spoke of the drought that had destroyed the crops; of the floods that had taken the dam out of the Virgin River time after time causing the crops to die. He spoke of the Indian raids; of the deaths that had been due to lack of milk for little children, and of the dread Black Canker and by the unpalatable plants eaten to keep off starvation. He reminded them that despite all they had endured, they had completed the Tabernacle and could [now] enjoy its blessings.

"'No wonder you people,' he said in substance, 'have had a hard time! No wonder this land has been a barren desert devoid of rainfall that has almost defied subjection! No wonder you have died of sickness and starvation! This land has been cursed by the mouth of God, because of the Gadianton Robbers that infested it in former days! And I say unto you my brethren and sisters, that this land is now infested with the spirits of those Gadianton Robbers! They are everywhere about you! They are hiding and peeping around corners at you! They are crowded around this Temple, those evil spirits, gnashing their teeth in anger that you have succeeded!

"'If you could draw aside the veil and see them, you would be afraid to leave this place and go to your homes.' Outside, as the meeting closed, a fierce storm had blown up. So great was the velocity of the wind that buggies were upset or blown cross country and horses were stampeded. Trees were uprooted and roofs were lifted off houses and carried away. The settlers looked fearfully at each other, lest they see the spirits of the Gadianton Robbers in the flesh. And [even] little children clung to their mothers' skirts crying in terror, even after they had reached their own houses [in relative safety]."

At various other times in his annual trips to Southern Utah from Salt Lake City, Brigham Young also identified other areas within the state which were former habitations for these Nephite mafia bands. He told a group of Saints in Manti once that "some of the Gadianton Robbers were in the vicinity of Sanpete [County in ancient times] looking for treasures of those [Jaredites] who came from the Tower [of Babel]. Salem, Payson, Santaquin, and Salina were also earmarked as other Gadianton hangouts (see Journal of Abraham H.

Cannon under the May 20th, 1894 entry). He indicated "that it would require very good Saints to live" in such places "and not lose the[ir] faith" on account of the hordes of evil spirits lurking in these different places. Cedar City and Fillmore also were filled with numerous wicked spirits "of the old Gadianton Robbers who infested these Mountains for more than a thousand years" (see Wilford Woodruff's Journal under the May 16th, 1851 and April 28th, 1867 entry dates).

But he wasn't the only one who could detect such unseen wicked influences. Apostle Francis M. Lyman was another Church General Authority blessed with a similar spirit of discernment. Bishop E. P. Pectol of Torrey, Utah contributed this piece of valuable information in *The Messenger* (3(7):83; April 28, 1909), an official publication of the New Zealand Mission of the Church when he apparently served there on a mission as a young man.

"A number of years ago, while visiting the Wayne Stake of Zion [in Wayne County], Apostle [Francis] Marion Lyman, standing near a meetinghouse after Sunday services, [seemed to be] apparently in deep thought. [He] raised his hand with a motion from west to east and made a declaration in words similar to the following:

"'The country we now behold was once the stronghold of a portion of the Gadianton Robbers spoken of in the Book of Mormon. Here their secret signs and combinations were planned, and from here they sallied forth to perpetrate their devilish deeds. Many of those spirits still inhabit those old haunts where they were wont to be in the flesh and influence men to the same deeds of wickedness.'

"This statement is somewhat strengthened when we understand that this section of country bordering the Colorado River has been infested by lawless bands ever since Mexico was conquered by the Spaniards. And in our time [it] has been the rendezvous of the notorious 'Hole in the Wall' and 'Robbers' Roost' gangs which have been a source of dread and annoyance, not only to stockmen and farmers but to railroad and commercial men as well. [These gangs] perpetrat[ed] similar deeds as were committed by the Gadianton Robbers, whether or not they have been carried [out] on the same grounds as were [those] influenced by [these] evil spirits. We are glad, however, that those gangs of marauders have been broken up and split asunder until not enough are left to carry on their depredations in the same bold way."

In James S. Brown's autobiographical work, *Giant of the Lord*: Life of A Pioneer (Salt Lake City: Bookcraft, Inc., 1960; p. 136), we find this warning given by Apostle Heber C. Kimball: "These mountains will be filled with robbers, highwaymen, and all kinds of thieves and murderers, for the spirit of the old Gadianton Robbers lurks here in the mountains, and will take possession of men, and you will have to watch as well as pray, to keep [them] away [from you]."

According to an article in *The Contributor* (15(5):317; March, 1894) magazine by H. E. Baker: "Near the close of the fourth century, the Nephite dominion extended from the Land of Zarahemla, now Venezuela and the eastern portion of Colombia, northwest through the Central American states and Mexico, through Texas, and up the valley of the Mississippi and its tributaries, and far into the east towards the Atlantic." The Diary of Charles Lowell Walker (Logan: Utah State University Press, 1980; 2:525-26) speaks of Gadiantons and others "travelling to Cumorah from the south and southwest" [and] of having to bury [some of] their treasures as they journeyed."

But the biggest stash of all their plundered loot, believe it or not, is right in the southern end of Utah County between the small communities of Salem and Payson. By some people's way of reckoning, there is probably enough gold squirreled away in those majestic mountains directly to the east to save the country from bankruptcy or the Kingdom of God from total financial ruin. It is a story worth telling and remembering, because ALL of it is TRUE! But some background information leading up to this may be helpful here.

My father Jacob Heinerman, my younger brother, Joseph, and I lived for several years on a small two-acre farm in Salem. At that time I was in the third grade and remember arguing with my schoolteacher, Mr. Thomas about the virtues of then Governor, J. Bracken Lee, who was almost universally despised by Utah teachers because of his ardent stand against giving them any more salary increases. While Mr. Thomas couldn't vent the anger in his spleen at me physically, yet he took it out on me in other ways, and my report card showed it even though I was one of the smartest and brightest kids in his class.

There also lived in Salem at that time an old Mormon apostate named Francis Michael Darter, whom we knew casually through various LDS Church books that my father periodically sold him. He was the author of three books on topics covering specific Biblical prophecies concerning the Latter-day Saints, the Last Days, the redemption of Zion, and the role of the Lamanites or Native Americans in the building of the Great Temple in Jackson County, MO during the Millennium. He wrote the first one, *The Time of The End* in 1928 while residing in Long Beach, California and serving a three-year stake mission there. The next volume *Our Bible in Stone* was written and published in 1931. The final volume in his "Restoration of Zion" trilogy series, *Zion's Redemption* came out in 1933 after he had relocated to Salt Lake City, where he labored as a civil engineer and surveyor.

Well before his book, however, Darter had contributed an important article to a major Church periodical the *Improvement Era* (19:33-43; November 1915), which then served as the official organ of all priesthood quorums, the Young Men's Mutual Improvement Association (YMMIA), and various church-sponsored schools. Great interest had been generated at the time among a number of different people as to the exact day on which the Lord was put to death. Through some of his rank-and-file priesthood leaders, who knew of his writing and research capabilities, Darter (then holding the office of Elder) was asked to prepare a lengthy treatise addressing this matter from a Mormon perspective. The result was "On What Day Was Jesus Christ Crucified?"

But like so many others before, during and since his time, Darter's pride eventually got the best of him. From the popularity that this one article and his three books drew, he became a favorite speaker at numerous Church "fireside" gatherings (as they were then called). While obviously doing good in some ways, yet he was also doing great disservice by letting his own opinions creep into his subject materials more and more. When his speculations superceded solid scriptures, he was called on the carpet for it and severely rebuked by lower-ranking Church ecclesiastical leaders.

His own great ego and self-importance prevented the man from humbling himself, acknowledging the error of his ways, and sincerely repenting of these mistakes. He withstood the reprimands and counsel given him, trying only to mount a sufficient defense of his own views. As punishment for his stubbornness, he was stripped of all Church callings and his ward bishop put on notice to monitor the man's actions more carefully. He continued giving lectures, though, on his favorite gospel themes to many Saints, but now did so in private homes instead of chapels.

There lived, in the 9th Ward at that time, a single woman named Bertha van Frantz, a convert from the Netherlands. My father Jacob Heinerman knew her quite well when he lived in this ward, being her home teacher at the time. She went to one of Darter's lectures and became fascinated with the things he said. They soon became very good friends and he eventually persuaded her to become his plural wife. Shortly after this, both of them were officially excommunicated from the Church.

They took up residency in Salem because Darter believed in the visions and prophecies of John Koyle, formerly a Mormon bishop of the Leland Ward, who was eventually excommunicated himself on April 1, 1948, for his continued involvement in what has become known as the Dream Mine. Darter took it upon himself to befriend the aged and disheartened Koyle and interviewed a number of his close associates relative to this mine and its mill against the side of the mountain just east of Salem. Darter and his plural wife Bertha managed to gain a lengthy interview with Koyle some time before his demise on May 17, 1949. A number of written questions were asked and numerous notes taken about the old man's visionary experiences concerning the mine itself.

After our family moved from Salem and relocated in Provo where my father then opened Cottage Book Shop, Darter still kept in contact, occasionally dropping by for short chit-chats or to purchase a book of some interest to him. At about this same time, my father, brother and I became acquainted with a young journalism student attending Brigham Young University. His name was Ted Wilde and he was an assistant editor of the campus student newspaper called the *Daily Universe*. My father ran a series of small block ads in the paper in hopes of enticing some students and professors to visit his bookstore. Wilde helped create some clever limericks for these ads that made them quite a hit with the paper's readers. Our family soon became good friends with the Wildes and were invited over for Sunday dinner at different times. Ted saw in my father the kind of qualities he wished his own dad would have had and soon "adopted" Jacob in a "father figure" role. He spent a great deal of time with my father, helping to fix an old Pontiac car and sometimes traveling with him when dad went out to private homes to make a book or antique purchase.

In hanging around the bookstore quite a bit, Ted eventually became acquainted with Darter. His interest in the Dream Mine and its possible contents came alive very quickly due to some of his conversations with this man. One week, when Darter and Bertha were in our bookstore and Ted was present with my father, an invitation was extended to visit the couple some evening at their home. Not long after this, my father, brother Joseph, myself and Ted Wilde drove to Salem in the blue Pontiac and spent almost four hours visiting the Darters. An old Wollensack tape recorder was brought along for the purpose of recording what Francis Michael said; I had borrowed it for the evening from one of my junior high school teachers.

The fascinating story that follows, regarding the origins of the Dream Mine, comes primarily from what Darter, and sometimes his plural wife Bertha, told the four of us that night based on first-hand information given to them by Bishop John Koyle shortly before his death. I've also incorporated a little additional data which Quayle Dixon of Spanish Fork provided me with some years ago; he was a close associate of Koyle's and after the man's death continued supervising mine business for many years until his own demise.

John Hyrum Koyle was born on August 14, 1864 in Spanish Fork, UT. He married Emily Arvilla Holt in 1884 and settled on a small farm to the south of that city in a place called Riverside (which later was renamed Leland). There he followed the honorable profession of farming and became "a tiller of the soil" and raiser of livestock. One time a favorite red heifer of his became lost and he hunted for her almost a month without any success. Then one night he had a dream in which he saw this animal standing in a field below some railroad tracks, facing east. The next morning he crossed the tracks and went to that particular field where he located his lost animal. This became a testimony to him that the Restored Gospel of Jesus Christ was true. From this moment on, he was blessed with the gift of dreams and visions and became somewhat of a noted seer within his own community and the mission field.

He surprised his wife one day by informing her that an angelic being had instructed him to go on a Church mission while he was out lowing his field. He served for several years in the Southern States Mission which was then presided over by President J. Golden Kimball, who served in that capacity from 1891 to 1893; Kimball was called to

99

the First Council of the Seventy in 1892 and set apart as a General Authority. At that time, this was the most dangerous mission in the entire Church, as people in the South held deep resentment towards all Latter-day Saints. A number of missionaries before this had been severely beaten, tarred and feathered and run out of town on a rail, nearly hanged until dead, or shot down like dogs in cold blood.

But the Lord was mindful of Koyle and always protected him and those companions who served with him. It was done through his unique gift of dreams in which he would always see the trouble and its final outcome before any of it had transpired. He always followed the information given to him in these visions of the night. It wasn't too long before Elder Kimball learned of these experiences and soon met the humble missionary who had them. He would himself become a benefactor of one of Koyle's dreams a lot sooner than even he realized.

Now a mission conference had been planned for some time in advance. The night before its occurrence, however, Koyle saw in a dream, that a large and unruly mob had gathered for the purpose of capturing J. Golden Kimball and holding him for ransom. In the dream, it seemed to Koyle that the mobocrats were only interested in this General Authority and no one else. A divine being appeared within the vision and informed him that if President Kimball canceled his appearance at the conference, his enemies would disperse from disappointment. Koyle informed his mission leader of these things the very next day. Kimball was himself a spiritual man and respected the spirituality of others. He heeded the dream's warning and didn't show up. The meeting took place as planned, a mob came and searched through the building, but not finding the man they came after, left without causing further problems. After his episode, Kimball told Koyle that if he ever got any more dreams in the future to so inform him of the same. A lifelong friendship sprang up between both men.

Upon his return home after filling an honorable mission, Koyle settled to his usual business of farming. He built a nice little side business by selling butter, homemade cheese and other farm produce to the mining towns of Mercur and Tintic a few miles southwest of where he lived. He befriended certain miners and on several occasions was invited to go into a few small mines and see for himself how they were managed. One night shortly after that, he saw in a dream a large deposit of valuable ore in one of the mountains near Tintic. He related

A distant view of Koyle Dream Mine and mill the
mountain in Salem, Utah

A close up view of the mill with the mine entrance just to the left of it.

this to his ward bishop, who told him it was a bunch of nonsense, all of the devil, and to leave well enough alone. But not long thereafter, a rich ore deposit was discovered by others and when fully mined out made them very wealthy people. At this point in his life, Koyle decided to put full faith in his gift of dreams, even though they might sometimes run contrary to the counsel of his Church leaders.

Then on the night of August 27th, 1894, the "Big One" happened, which would forever change the rest of his life. He received what one might call "the Mother of all mining dreams!" No one before him or since then ever had anything similar that has had such a profound impact on the lives of tens of thousands of otherwise ordinary, spiritually-average but good-hearted Latter-day Saints. And boy, was it a doozy, to say the least.

Throughout his life, John Koyle recited this one dream hundreds and hundreds of times, always with the same clarity and exactness to details. Obviously, though, with each retelling of the classic "fish-that-got-away" story, the fish becomes a little bigger each time. But that problem lay more with the listeners of Koyle's tale than with the old man himself. That's what convinced Francis and Bertha Darter to go and pay him a visit and get the story straight from the one who had actually experienced it first-hand. Being an engineer and surveyor, Darter was a stickler for detail and asked those types of questions that would pinpoint certain details of the Dream Mine account with greater accuracy and devoid of any added embellishments by zealous disciples' of Koyle.

On the night of August 27th, 1894, Koyle was in bed but had a difficult time falling asleep. After a while, his tossing and turning ceased and a sudden, unexpected calm descended over him. A large personage dressed in drab gray apparel appeared before him. He informed the startled Koyle that he had been foreordained in the Pre-Existent World to come to earth and be an important instrument in the discovery of an ancient lost treasure located nearby that would someday be used for rescuing the floundering American economy and, more particularly, to save the Church itself from ultimate bankruptcy.

This unusual individual touched Koyle's body and the man found himself in spirit form a few seconds later. They proceeded to travel through the air at lightning speed to a mountain east of Salem, where they were able to penetrate the solid rock with considerable ease. His guide showed him an unmistakable cream-colored mineral leader that wended its way down into the heart of the mountain. This leader culminated a thousand feet below the surface at a very hard capstone, beneath which lay a very large body of rich, white quartz chock full of leaf gold. Both continued making their way down another 175 feet through this chimney of rich ore to a vast body of gold ore that had been mined out in ancient times and smelted down into different forms of gold bullion. Koyle counted nine large caverns in which these operations had once taken place. Huge pillars standing in the middle of each room supported the earth overhead from collapsing. Koyle informed the Darters that they made far better tunnel supports anciently than miners did today.

Koyle was totally awed by the wealth he saw in all those rooms. It exceeded everything his own mind would have been capable of imagining. Gold was everywhere to be found–in piles of neatly stacked gold bars, in large jars and vases full of minted gold coins, and in other relics such as drinking goblets, crowns, rings, writs and ankle amulets, earrings, and other personal jewelry. There were also a number of swords with gold hilts and inlaid with precious and semi-precious stones, golden shields, gold-tipped spears, gold vestments and even gilded armor.

While the guide stood by off to one side, Koyle's spirit wandered around in obvious shock; he felt like the poor kid who had just entered the largest toy store on earth and had complete access to all of its inventory for a few hours. He reported noticing a number of gold-plated records with strange hieroglyphics on them, which he was told contained individual histories of many of the ancient inhabitants of the Americas.

Now there were a number of different publications over the years which have told of this same experience and given other detailed history concerning the origins, operations, and present status of Koyle's Relief Mine or Dream Mine. These include several books by apostate writers: Norman C. Pierce's *The Dream Mine Story* (1972); Ogden Kraut's two works, John H. Koyle's *Relief Mine and Relief Mine II: Through Others' Eyes* (both by Pioneer Press of Salt Lake City, 1978 and 1998 respectively). Also there are two student theses on the subject as well: James R. Christianson's "An Historical Study of the Koyle Relief Mine, 1894-1962" (Master's thesis, BYU, 1962); and Joe

The road beyond the locked gate that leads to the Dream Mine operation. This was apparently the major site where the Gadianton Robbers stashed most of their plundered Nephite wealth in ancient *Book of Mormon* times.

The slag dump just to the left of the mill sits in front of the mine entrance itself. A locked gate covers a tunnel that runs back deep into the mountain for a few thousand feet.

Stanley Graham's "The Dream Mine: A Study in Mormon Folklore" (Master's thesis, BYU, 1970). All of these have numerous recountings of the Koyle dream in which the spiritual messenger is identified as being from heaven and thought to be Moroni or one of the resurrected Three Nephites. Francis Darter pointedly asked Koyle during his interview of the man if, in fact, the visitor had ever given his name or specifically where he came from. Koyle thought a moment and replied that, come to think of it, he never actually did identify himself or his place of origin. Koyle honestly admitted that he just assumed the fellow was Moroni and that he came from Heaven. He said he was able to shake hands with the man, though, which is intriguing considering that Koyle was then just a disembodied spirit. Mormon doctrine clearly teaches that mortal beings can never physically shake hands with spirits, nor can those temporarily disembodied spirits do the same with actual resurrected beings, who themselves possess physical bodies of flesh and bone. Undoubtedly then, Koyle's visitor was in spirit form at the time, just as he was, which explains why the two spirits were able to shake hands like they did.

These other reference works also quote a number of informants as telling them that this strange visitor spent a great deal of time with Koyle in the mining details connected with the intended excavation of this unfathomable wealth. But the Darters stated that Koyle's visitor spent more time telling him how this large and diversified booty had been acquired. He said it came from numerous expeditions all over the Nephite empire and had been collected there in this repository for safe-keeping and storage. Darter reasoned that the wealth had been stolen, for the most part, and secreted in this particular location by the Gadianton Robbers of old. He wouldn't go so far, though, as to identify Koyle's visitor as Gadianton himself, but speculated that the unidentified personage may have been "one of the more benevolent-minded robbers" of this very ancient mafia-like brotherhood.

"The rest of the story," as radio newsman Paul Harvey of Chicago was fond of saying, may be read in any one of the aforementioned titles. Koyle spread his story, gathering about himself men of all economic classes and education—many came from mediocre backgrounds, but a few were better-educated and well-off than the rest. They dug long tunnels into the hill in hopes of finding something. An expensive mill was built adjacent to it on mine property. But for all those thousands of Saints who invested untold dollars and exercised a great deal of faith in this project and its promoters, great disappointment was to become their loss, as no gold of any kind has ever been found within that Salem mountain. Still, even for a pragmatist like Darter, he felt that there was something inside the mountain of unspecified value; but that it had been ill gotten.

There is a further clue to suggest that spiritual affairs of this Dream Mine are guided by the forces of darkness rather than light. Church President Joseph F. Smith condemned the mine and Apostle James E. Talmage, a geologist by profession who investigated it thoroughly, calling it a ruse, both appeared at separate times to Koyle in dreams of the night, "begging and asking his forgiveness for their opposition to it." Those few who have good spiritual discernment with them, who have been to the mine property in times past, can testify that an unpleasant spirit broods over the whole place and has given them uneasy feelings whenever they've gone there.

My own father Jacob Heinerman had an indirect experience with some of the public stock that was sold in the Dream Mine many years ago for $3.00 a share. There lived on the corner of Bryan Avenue and 800 East in Salt Lake City in the 1940s, a German emigrant convert woman by the name of Sister Sarr. She lived in the same Bryan Ward that my parents did and attended my father's Gospel Doctrine class on a fairly regular basis. Dad would often visit her in the capacity of doing good for the widows and orphans living in the ward at that time. While not exactly poor, she was a person of some financial means, earning her income by giving people sweat-bath treatments in her large two-storied Victorian-style home.

Sister Sarr liked my father very much and didn't care at all for my mother Jennie. Being up in her years at the time and having no close family relatives nearby, she decided to have her lawyer draw up a will, deeding everything over to my father upon her death. She informed him of her intentions one time and showed him 25,000 shares of Dream Mine stock which was in her possession. Dad felt an uncomfortable spirit come over him upon seeing all of these stock certificates laid out on the table before him. He graciously declined her kind offer. Still, she kept insisting that he let her do this, but the harder she pushed, the more uneasy he became about the whole matter. In the end, he got up, bid her farewell and walked out of her house. In looking

Caretaker and guard residences and administrative offices at the entrance of the Gadianton treasure mine against Salem mountain.

Looking out across the southwest end of Utah County from the mine entrance.

back on that incident many years later, he felt it was the Dream Mine stock itself that gave him the willies, rather than Sarr, whom he described as being "typically German" with her stubbornness and high-mindedness, but still "a pretty good old soul" at that. She eventually passed on, but whatever became of her stock was never known.

A few years later, while dad was in Sam Weler's Zion Bookstore in downtown Salt Lake City, he met a fellow by the name of Heber T. ("H.T.") Hanks, who at one time worked at the mine in 1947-48, before eventually becoming affiliated with the Order of Aaron apostate sect in the Utah west desert. "H.T" brought up the subject of the Dream Mine and dad related to him this experience with Sister Sarr. Hanks refused to believe it, saying that no one, not even Koyle himself, ever possessed that large a block of stock. But then after reflecting upon the matter for a few minutes, Hanks apologized to my father and acknowledged that such a thing was highly possible. He said that during the 1940s when a flurry of activity had resumed at the mine, that there arose at one time a sudden need for a quick influx of cash from somewhere. Some of Koyle's intimate associates "beat the bushes" trying to find someone either stupid or willing enough (or both) to donate some money to their imagined cause. Word came to them about this Sister Sarr in Salt Lake and an anxious path was hurriedly beat to her doorstep in search of more funds. Sarr listened to their story and agreed to let them have some money, but not the entire amount they were seeking. But it came with one condition: In exchange for her investment, she was to receive a great deal more stock than the actual monies she gave out. Nothing like this had ever been done before, but due to the desperate nature of the situation at hand, they reluctantly agreed to her demands; this is how she ended up with 25,000 shares of common stock.

On Tuesday, May 8th, 2000 the annual meeting of Dream Mine shareholders and directors met as usual in the Veteran's Memorial Hall in Spanish Fork. About 75 people were in attendance, including Mormon fundamentalist Ogden Kraut. The meeting only lasted about 20 minutes and was conducted by the aging Board of Directors. A report on mine income and outgoing expenses was given by the treasurer, followed by some other business and then a closing prayer. A question-and-answer session followed afterwards. It was announced in the meeting that a woman had 100 shares of Dream Mine stock for sale and wanted $10 per share for it. It was snatched up immediately by someone of obvious affluence within the audience. Just a year before that, another shareholder's stock had gone for $7.00 each. Kraut joked with me in a phone call that if my father had taken Sarr up on her generous offer back then, "today your father could retire in style."

Many years ago I spoke with the late Austin E. Fife, an ethnologist at Utah State University who specialized in the study and collection of folklore. He mentioned that "a number of other Utah communities have had their own John Koyles and dream mine ventures."

There was another Mormon bishop, Ben Bullock of the Bonneville Ward in Provo (and a friend of Koyle's, too), who was given an open vision while plowing his field in 1915 sometime. He saw an enormous chamber filled with "all types of gold piled nearly to the ceiling" thereof. He was informed by a presumed "heavenly" messenger that "the money was to be used to build up the Kingdom of God, to gather the righteous to Zion, and to feed and house the Saints during a time of great famine." Bullock claimed that John Koyle visited him in a dream on the night of February 13, 1957, telling him that "those who were operating his Dream Mine were not doing a satisfactory job" and that he, Bullock, had been chosen to excavate another hidden mine east of Santaquin where much plundered wealth lay secreted for many centuries. He spent a number of decades and a small fortune in the process to develop the Bullock Tunnel but nothing ever came of these efforts.

That there is something to and inside the Dream Mine in Salem cannot be disputed. That public awareness was created of this by mischievous spirits to tantalize the greedy and those weak in faith with "visions" of elusive riches that never will materialize is a definite certainty. That any of the mountain's buried contents will ever be used to rescue the Church from eventual bankruptcy remains to be seen. But if and whenever such grand treasures are ever hauled forth, rest assured that federal agents of the Internal Revenue Service will be at the mine entrance with extended arms and open hands demanding to receive their pound of flesh!

The following inspired ditty pretty much sums up what the Koyle Dream Mine in Salem, Utah and its Gadianton stash of untold wealth is all about:

"Dream on! Dream on!" Investors keep
Their hopes up in those treasures deep,
While behind the Vail robbers laugh
At the attention given such gaff.

"Poor silly mortals," they like to say,
"Can't see the fun we're having today;
'Tis better than when we plundered loot–
To see their vexings gives us a hoot!"

"And makes our stay in Hell worthwhile
So long as we can always beguile
Those numbskulls who think they'll become rich
Someday with property we bewitch!"

CHAPTER NINE

TECHNOLOGICAL WEALTH OF THE ANCIENTS–PRE-FLOOD AND POST-FLOOD CONSEQUENCES

On August 13, 1521, the last Aztec ruler of Tenochtitlan surrendered to the "bloody butcher" Spanish conquistador Hernan Cortes at Tlatelolco in the northern part of the Aztec capital in Mexico. Soon thereafter a determination was made that these heathen Aztecs needed Christianizing in order to save their own poor pagan souls from the devil idolatry in which they were heavily steeped. Between 1524 and 1533, three Catholic orders of friars – the Franciscans, the Dominicans, and the Augustinians – came from Spain to the New World for this very purpose. No slack was cut for any Aztecs who wished to stick with their old heathen beliefs and ways – they were summarily executed on orders from the friars.

There came also from Spain to Mexico, with one of these missionary groups, a young child, Diego Duran, with his family. His father held a position of some importance in the Spanish colonial government. The boy witnessed numerous Aztec slaves being branded in the homes of his relatives; this event played a great role in his decision to become a priest when he grew up so that he might help alleviate some of the suffering and terrible injustices then being regularly imposed on the subdued natives by their cruel conquerors. In his late teens he entered the Dominican Order as a novice, later to become a deacon in the convent there.

Awhile after this he was dispatched to the convento at Oaxtepec, where he was influenced by "a most honest priest," who is thought to have been Fray Francisco de Aguilar. Aguilar had been a soldier under Cortes before entering the Dominican Order and had much to tell young Duran about the conquest. Duran speaks frequently of him in his *History of the Indies of New Spain* (Norman, OK:

University of Oklahoma Press, 1994). Aguilar himself had experienced a gradual change of heart while still a conquistador and felt sympathetic towards the Aztecs; by entering the Catholic priesthood he hoped it might, in part, atone for some of his previous sins committed against the oppressed people while still a soldier. It was Aguilar, in fact, who helped to greatly expand in young Fray Duran the kindly feelings and respect for the Aztecs which he had felt as a child. Aguilar wisely counseled him to seek out those elderly informants who knew something of the history of these people and interview them with the idea of keeping a written record of what they knew before it became permanently lost upon their deaths.

Some time later, Fray Duran received an appointment from his superiors in Mexico City to become the vicar in Hueyapan, a town high on the southern slopes of the volcano Popocatepetl; the Dominican convento there dates from 1563 and is still in use today. In that Nahuatl-speaking region Duran found numerous informants for his eventual History. His fluency in the native tongue of the Aztecs was learned as a child and served him well while stationed there. One of the important characteristics of his research is that he ventured into rural areas, questioning the old and young in their own language, observing their customs, and always searching for ancient documents, which he felt could parallel some of the more ancient history of mankind that is found in Genesis of the Old Testament. In his search for such evidence and in concert with his daily missionary work among the native people, he discovered pictorial manuscripts that he incorporated into his History; unfortunately these and old native maps also acquired were not preserved as they should have been. No other friar of the time, not even the more famous Franciscan Father Bernardino de Sahugun, whose own encyclopedic account of Aztec culture is without compare, could match this priest's wide access to the natives or their readily-gained trust so fully.

Diego Duran was particularly interested in the very old Aztec legends having to do with the great Tower of Babel, that was in ancient times located in the alluvial plains of Shinar situated between the Tigris and Euphrates rivers, where the Sumerian civilization began in what is now the southern part of Iraq. Jewish legends had it that "the builders of the Tower" were incensed that "the people of the upper world" enjoyed a greater advantage than those "left in the lower world" and, therefore, determined to erect a structure high enough to visit them" (see *The Jewish Encyclopedia* (New York: Funk and Wagnalls Co., 1903; 2:396).

Fray Duran came across one very elderly Aztec gentleman who was able to recall with vivid clarity the traditions about the Tower of Babel which had been handed among his people over many successive generations. Here in Duran's own words is a narrative of that amazing account:

"An aged man from Cholula, about one hundred years old, began to describe their [Aztec] origins to me. This man, who because of his great age walked bent over toward the earth, was quite learned in their ancient traditions. When I begged him to enlighten me about some details I wished to put into this history, he asked me what I wanted him to tell. I realized I had found an old and learned person, so I answered, all that he knew about the history of his Indian nation from the beginning of the world. He responded: 'Take pen and paper, because you will not be able to remember all that I shall tell you.' And began thus–

"'In the beginning, before light or sun had been created, this world lay in darkness and shadows and was void of every living thing. It was all flat, without a hill or ravine, surrounded on all sides by water, without even a tree or any other created thing. And then, when the light and sun were born in the east, men of monstrous stature appeared and took possession of this country. These giants, desirous of seeking the birth of the sun and its setting, decided to seek [dawn and dusk], and they separated into two groups. One band walked toward the west and the other toward the east. The latter walked until the sea cut off their route; from here they decided to return to the place from which they had set out, called Iztac Zolin Inemian [means 'Where White Quails Dwell'].

"'Not having found a way to teach the sun but enamored of its light and beauty, they decided to build a tower so high that its summit would reach unto heaven. And gathering materials for this building, the giants found clay for bricks and an excellent mortar with which they began to build the tower very swiftly. When they had raised it as high as they could – and it seemed to reach to heaven – the Lord of the Heights became angry and said to the inhabitants of the heavens, 'Have you seen that the men of the earth have built a proud and lofty tower in order to come up here, enamored as they are of the light of the sun and its beauty? Come, let us confound them, for it is not right that these earthlings, made of flesh, mingle with us.' Then swift as lightning those who dwell in the heavens came out from the four regions of the world and tore down the tower that had been constructed. And the giants, bewildered and filled with terror, separated and fled in all directions.

"'That is how [this] Indian relate[d] the creation of the world with giants and the tower of Babel. Therefore, I am convinced and wish to convince others that those who tell this account heard it from their ancestors; and these natives belong, in my opinion, to the lineage of the chosen people of God for whom He worked great marvels. And so [a] knowledge of the things told in the Bible and its mysteries have passed from hand to hand, from father to son [over many long generations].'"

Similar legends exist about the great Tower in other parts of Mexico. Edward King Kingsborough, a British lord and man of some considerable means, spent his entire fortune in publishing over a period of 17 years (1831-1848) a massive nine-volume folio set entitled, *Antiquities of Mexico*. The end result of all his efforts and a printing and binding bill exceeding one million dollars was a giant repository of facsimiles of many ancient Aztec scrolls, maps, paintings, and parchments filled with hieroglyphics that were locked away in storage in a number of the world's great museums and private libraries, which the general public and most scholars were denied access to. Unfortunately, Lord Kingsborough died penniless in debtor's prison and a broken-hearted man because of this; but we are the benefactors of his excessive zeal in this regard.

From this huge work (8:25;27) comes the following legend about Babel from the Mexican state of Chiapas:

"An ancient manuscript of the primitive Indians of that province, who had learned the art of writing, had retained the constant tradition that the father and founder of their nation was Teponahuale, which signifies, 'Lord of the hollow piece of wood [or barge].' And that he was present at the building of the Great Wall, for so they named the Tower of Babel. And beheld with his own eyes the confusion of tongues. After which event, God, the Creator, commanded him to come to these extensive regions, and to divide them among mankind.

116

Some of the gold plates taken from the old Jaredite burial chamber in southcentral Utah and kept in a bank deposit box for safe-keeping.

They affirm that at the time of the confusion of tongues, there were seven families who spoke the same language, which was Nahuatl, that which is still spoken by the Aztec Mexicans. And since they understood each other, they united and, forming a single company, proceeded on their journey through diverse lands and countries as chance directed them, and without any particular destination in search of a convenient habitation. And having traveled during a century, passing in the interval mountains, rivers and arms of the sea, which they noted down in their paintings, they arrived at the place which they named their first settlement. [It was] in the Northern part of this kingdom, which they named Tlapaln, which signifies red country, on account of the soil being of that color."

These are but two examples which are typical of the many different Native American legends concerning the great Tower in Central Asia and some of those who eventually emigrated from there to the Western Hemisphere. Those who are familiar with The Book of Mormon know that the entire Book of Ether covers this particular period of time and those who made such a departure. In fact, a careful reading of the two previous Indian legends with the short account given of the same facts in the opening chapters of Ether, will discover many overlapping similarities between each of the accounts.

In a public sermon given on October 8th, 1860 in the old Bowery on Temple Square in Salt Lake City, President Brigham Young alluded to the many wonderful treasures brought from the Tower of Babel by the first people who resettled this part of the world shortly after the Flood (see Journal of Discourses 8:209): "Were the Lord to reveal to me where the ancient Jaredites hid their hundred of millions of dollars' worth of treasure, I should not take it and hand it out to the people, unless the Lord directed me to do so. Otherwise, it would perhaps seal the damnation of many; for at present you are better off without those treasures than you would be with them."

This author was privileged many years ago to befriend a man who had, indeed, stumbled across several caches and caves containing some of the fantastic wealth of these ancient inhabitants. In time he was able to earn enough of the man's trust and confidence to be taken to not one but two large caves filled with relics, artifacts, and mummies that would stagger the imagination for sure. From what was seen, handled and eventually brought out of both caves by the author and his guide, I would have to whole-heartedly agree with Brigham's estimate of "hundred of millions of dollars'" in terms of this buried treasures' value. But, if those figures are revised at what today's gold objects fetch on the open market, then it would definitely have to be "tens of BILLIONS of dollars' worth of treasure." (More about this in the next chapter.)

But gold, silver, precious stones, and so forth are pretty heady stuff for most people to be able to handle in a responsible way. Usually Satan will enter their hearts some way and grab hold of their minds, thereby creating a common form of spiritual epilepsy known as GREED! This has always been a trouble for most people since time immemorial. As was pointed out in a previous chapter on the wealth in the Hill Cumorah, even someone as good and noble and pure as what young Joseph Smith was, can (and did) easily succumb to the bright lure of beautiful gold. It is truly an irresistible temptation for most.

The man who found some of Babel's buried cave treasures in south central Utah many years ago learned this lesson the hard way. This author was provided a photocopy of the private journal of John Brewer of Moroni, Utah some time back when the two of them had become the best of friends. Long before the man's own prayer was answered that someone be brought into his life whom he could actually trust (which was the sole reason for our totally unexpected meeting), Brewer had put rightful confidence in the wrong kind of people. His entry for April 26, 1856 is offered in evidence of this very thing:

"I brought a guy by the name of Gail McCaffery up to the cave but I didn't show it to him for I didn't quite trust him. I put it to him in such a way that he had a good idea what I had. I went one way and he another and I went into the treasure cave and I took the gold plate out and showed him and he then believed what I had told him. I made him swear to tell no one and he said that he would not. But I will wait and see if he keeps his word, and if he does, maybe I'll let him in on the rest of it. If I see that he doesn't keep his word, I'll just let him think that I am letting him go with me. I'll watch him and see if he comes up to the cave or around it. Then I'll know whether or not to trust him."

Brewer didn't have long to wait. Under his journal entry of April 29 is found these notations:

"I didn't have long to wait, for he came up today and brought

The top and bottom portions of a relatively plain stone box excavated from a ground cache somewhere in Sanpete County in
southcentral Utah. Though barely discernible, there are figures of a
centipede (inside upper lid) and a scorpion (inside bottom part)
inscribed on both sections of this stone box. Such images are believed to
have been ancient priesthood symbols of some sort.

An assortmenet of different artifacts excavated from an old Jaredite mound in Sanpete Valley in southcentral Utah.

someone else with him. But I didn't know the person that was with him but I'll try to find out who he is. I should have known better. You just can't trust anyone. It sure makes me mad at them and myself for letting someone in on this, for all they want is the money end of it. I met him down in Rick's Café and I talked to him and I asked where he had been. And he said that he had just gotten back from Mt. Pleasant. I had hoped to see the guy that was with him but it seemed that he was alone. I found out that he drank a lot so I didn't put any more trust in him."

The following day he made these diary observations: "I went to the treasure cave and hid it so that no one would find it, only me. I will have to be more careful from this day on for there will be Gail watching all the time. Boy, I must be awfully dumb to pick up a partner like that. Never again will I trust anyone until I['ve] put them to the test. I then went over west to do a little arrowhead hunting and to think things out. I must think of a way to get rid of Gail. He is a good person but this belongs to the Lord and I don't want it to fall into the wrong hands for they will use it wrong. They will even hide it for themselves so I am back at it alone again."

When the time came that this author eventually connected up with John Brewer at the Moroni Sewage Treatment Plant where he then worked, listened to his story and became convinced in my own mind that it was true, two very remarkable things occurred at that initial visit that caused him to seriously ponder on this particular visit. First, I told Brewer that the two mummies he spoke of in the old cave were Jaredites. The man's eyes grew large and he immediately snapped, "I didn't say that; how do you know this is so?" I shrugged and said, "By inspiration, how else?" I also informed him that I knew some of the relics in his treasure cave had been brought across the ocean a long time ago from the Tower of Babel. He just about arose out of his chair on hearing that statement. "You seem to know a lot about something you've never physically seen or actually been to." My simple reply was something to the effect of, "It's called the influence of the Holy Spirit and for me it's no big deal" (meaning, of course, the easy manner in which this unsought inspiration had come).

The second, more defining thing, that really riveted the man's attention on me long after we departed was that I never once asked him for a private, guided tour of his treasure cave as everyone else had done before me. I felt content enough with what I had heard, knew it was all true, and didn't need anything else to satisfy my soul that night. I drove on to Manti where my family and I then resided, thanking my Heavenly Father in my heart for His loving-kindness in bringing this event about in the strange way He did.

I became John Brewer's FRIEND, plain and simple. Not because the guy knew the location of several treasure caves, but because I saw in him certain good qualities that I admired and liked. In the course of time, as we associated together in different capacities, we became close friends. Finally, after Brewer had tested my loyalty and trustworthiness in different ways, I told him one day to his face: "John you don't have to play these kind of games with me. I'm your friend irrespective of what you have or know the whereabouts of. If it is your intention to take me to one or both of these caves someday, fine, well and good. If not, that is also perfectly fine. But you need to know that I don't want and don't care to go. It's your call on these matters, but please cease from further testing as it is making me somewhat weary."

The time came, however, when he finally made the decision to do so. And my life was never the same after that upon entering that first, older cave. What I can say from all that I saw and handled in the space of an hour or more is that the Jaredites came from a civilization that had incredible technology beyond my wildest dreams. This, for me, was much more exciting than piles of gold plates stacked around the room and kept in stone boxes or large clay jars filled with precious and semi-precious stones. Imagine, if you will, crawling into an ancient cave somewhere in south-central Utah and finding remnants of what had once been a primitive dry cell battery. Or finding enough evidence of electroplating technology dating back some 3,000 years or more. Or, how about this...glass objects made at a time when scientists say there wasn't the know-how of such things yet.

For myself as a scientist, these were the real finds and TRUE TREASURES! That the Jaredites came from ancient Sumer cannot be in the least bit doubted, for the older of the two caves proves that many times over. Arthur C. Custance was correct when he declared in his book *Genesis and Early Man* (Grand Rapids, MI: Zondervan Publishing House, 1975; p. 101) that the technology of the ancient Sumerians "had achieved a level of technical proficiency greater than that to be found in many parts of Europe just prior to the Industrial Revolution."

But don't take my word for it; let other references speak for themselves. Hans E. Wulff mentioned in *Technology and Culture Science* (7(4):499-501; Fall 1966) that stone and metal tumbler locks are "of great antiquity... dating back to about 2000 B.C.," being found even "in the ruins of ancient Nineveh." Or how about John B. Carlson's evidence in support of magnetic compasses being used 4,000 years ago by the ancient Chinese and the Mexican Olmecs (the archaeological name for the Jaredites) (see *Science* 189(4205):753-60; September 5, 1975). And get this: there were fully developed copper smelting and copper soldering industries already in place before the big Tower project was commenced, with available tools such as metal saws and chisels for woodwork and stonework (see *American Anthropologist* 69:145-161; 1967).

One need look no further than the Sumerian culture itself to find not only an advanced technology but also an equally high social order in place at the time that the Great Tower was under construction. In his book, *The Sumerians* (Chicago: University of Chicago Press, 1963; pp. 88;288-91) historian Samuel Noah Kramer discussed the some 360,000 inhabitants of Ur (the capital of Sumer) enjoying "the potter's wheel, the wheeled vehicle, the sailboat," highly developed metallurgy, amazing "architectural techniques" that included 'stone foundations and platforms, niched cells, painted walls, mosaic-covered columns, and impressive facades," not to mention a decimal system of mathematics and a flourishing literary output to rival that of the Greeks at least 1,500 years later. Furthermore, illiteracy was virtually non-existent, as even the most common citizens had easy and ready access to free education from the many libraries, academies and vocational schools that dominated the intellectual and industrial landscapes then.

In an early work by the same author, *History Begins At Sumer* (Philadelphia: University of Pennsylvania Press, 1956) are listed "39 firsts in recorded history" accomplished by these people. Kramer described these very gifted, highly talented, and definitely practical people as being the "first true geniuses" upon who's works all later Old World civilizations were built. Long before the political assemblies in "democratic" Greece and republican Rome came into being, there was a political "congress" patterned similarly to our own American Congress around 3000 B.C., which then consisted "of two 'houses'; a 'senate,' or an assembly of elders; and a 'lower house,' or an assembly of arms-bearing male citizens. It was a 'war congress,' called together to take a stand on the momentous question of war and peace; it had to choose between what we would describe as 'peace at any price' or war and independence. The 'senate,' with its conservative elders, declared for peace at all cost, but its decision was 'vetoed' by the king, who then brought the matter before the 'lower house.' This body declared for war and freedom, and the king approved." Except for the position of kingship, doesn't the rest of this ancient political scenario sound a lot like a page taken out of our own American political system?

The first governmental agency established especially for the collection of taxes was instituted at Sumer. And, like with our own Internal Revenue Service (IRS) here, things eventually got out of hand and numerous abuses were frequently reported. As a result, "a new and god-fearing ruler came to power who restored justice and freedom to the long-suffering citizens. From one end of the land to the other...there were no tax collector[s] [anymore]." This is the world's first known case of tax reduction, but it only lasted a decade before things returned to normal and it was "business as usual" again.

Sumerians enjoyed a form and practice of law that has uncanny parallels with our own present legal system. "A murder was committed in the land of Sumer in 1850 B.C. or thereabouts. Three men – a barber, a gardener, and one whose occupation is not known – killed a temple official. The murderers, for some unstated reason, then informed the victim's wife that her husband had been killed. Strangely enough, she kept their secret and did not notify the authorities. The crime was brought to the attention of [the king] and he turned the case over for trial to the Citizens Assembly which acted as a court of justice.

"In this assembly, nine men arose to prosecute the accused. They argued that not only the three actual murderers, but the wife as well, should be executed, presumably because she had remained silent after learning of the crime and could thus be considered an accessory after the fact. Two men in the assembly then spoke up in defense of the woman. They pleaded that the woman had taken no part in the murder of her husband, and that she should therefore go unpunished.

"The members of the assembly agreed with the defense. They

argued that the woman was not unjustified in remaining silent, since it seemed that her husband had failed to support her. Their verdict concluded with the statement that 'the punishment of those who actually killed should suffice.' Accordingly, only the three men were condemned by the assembly to be executed.

"The record of this murder trial was found inscribed in the Sumerian language on a clay tablet that was dug up in 1950 by a joint expedition of the Oriental Institute of the University of Chicago and the University Museum of the University of Pennsylvania. After [a] translation had been made [of the cuneiform inscriptions], it seemed relevant to compare the verdict with what the modern decision might have been in a similar situation. Therefore the translation [was sent] to the late Owen J. Roberts, then Dean of the Law School, University of Pennsylvania (he had been associate justice of the United States Supreme Court, 1930-45), and asked his opinion. His answer was of great interest, for in this legal case modern judges would have agreed with the Sumerian judges of long ago, and the verdict would have been the same. To quote Justice Roberts, 'The wife would not be guilty as an accessory after the fact under our law. An accessory after the fact must not only know that the felony was committed, but must also receive, relieve, comfort, or assist the felon [in some way].'"

Besides the benefits of a fair and just legal system, ancient Sumerians were also treated by doctors who practiced a strict form of medicine in the very beginning that was entirely devoid of magic and other superstitious nonsense. The world's "oldest medical handbook known to man, lay buried in [Sumerian city] ruins for more than 4,000 years, until it was excavated by an American expedition and brought to the University Museum in Philadelphia." The unknown Sumerian physician who wrote upon this clay tablet, measuring three and three fourths by six and one fourth inches in size, composed "his more valuable medical prescriptions." This ancient document shows that this doctor "went to botanical, zoological, and mineralogical sources for his *materia medica*," just like his modern counterpart does today. The remedies prescribed toward the end of the third millennium B.C. "were both salves and filtrates to be applied externally, and liquids to be taken internally. Salves were made by pulverizing one or more samples, then infusing the powder with wine, and finally spreading several tree oils over the mixture. The filtrate prescriptions, on the other hand, were far more complicated and accompanied by directions for treatment. An indirect but "broad acquaintance with quite a number of rather elaborate chemical operations and procedures" is certainly implied from the tablet's contents. Such filtrates were either employed externally or, more often, mixed with beer and administered internally. "It is interesting to note that the Sumerian physician who wrote [this] tablet did not resort to magic spells and incantations. Not one god or demon is mentioned anywhere throughout the text."

The foregoing was just the drug therapy portion of medical treatment in those times. The surgical side of things was also quite advanced as well. But proof of this comes not from Sumer, but rather from the Western Hemisphere and the Olmec culture, or its Jaredite equivalent around 1000 B.C. A 4.5-inch-high ceramic figure was excavated holding a human heart in its hands. What's most surprising about this unique find, though, is that it depicts the aorta, on the right, the pulmonary artery, and both ventricles. It is believed to be the earliest anatomically accurate image of a human heart, though older Egyptian hieroglyphs show similar features. Not until the 16th century did artists again achieve such detail (see *National Geographic*, March 1998, "Geographica" section). When this author was in the older cave several times with John Brewer in Sanpete County in south-central Utah, there were several objects that looked very much like some of the medical instruments which cardiologists would utilize to perform open-heart surgeries or do coronary bypasses with.

The world's first glass fish aquarium was built in Sumer by some unidentified individual, who, according to Kramer, "for one reason or another was an ardent lover of fish." Now it has been known for quite some time that fishing activity and a thriving fishing industry were already in place and served as a major source of Sumer's food supply, especially during construction of the Great Tower on the plains of Shinar. The single cuneiform clay tablet, appropriately called by archaeologists the "Home of the Fish" document, "begins with a reassuring announcement that the speaker has built a house for the fish, large, spacious, and unapproachable, and provided it with fine food and drink, especially beer and sweet cookies." The speaker then urges his friends and acquaintances to join him in his "house of fish" and watch various live specimens swim around, while enjoying the food, snacks, and free beer and wine provided for that occasion.

The Book of Mormon relates of a similar portable aquarium being constructed by the Jaredites at the time they were told to abandon their residences near the Tower of Babel and venture forth into the wilderness under the guiding influence of God. "And they did also prepare a vessel, in which they did carry with them the fish of the rivers" (see Ether 2:2). That ancient "Home of the Fish" tablet mentions sixteen different fish, only a few of which can be described with some reasonable degree of certainty – the carp, the sturgeon, the catfish, and the trout. It can be assumed that their presence in the water of North and South America was ultimately due to the Jaredites, since before their arrival here there apparently were no fish at all in any of the numerous lakes, rivers, and streams.

Above anything else the Sumerians were great agriculturists. It was they who gave us the world's first "Farmer's Almanac" before anyone else did. An American archaeological expedition digging in Iraq in 1949-50, found a three by four inch clay tablet covered with cuneiform inscriptions. After the artifact was baked, cleaned, and mended in a university museum laboratory in Philadelphia, practically its entire text became legible enough to be read and deciphered.

Kramer states in his *History Begins At Sumer* that "the restored document, 108 lines in length, consists of a series of instructions addressed by a farmer to his son for the purpose of guiding him throughout his yearly agricultural activities, beginning with the inundation of the fields in May-June and ending with the cleaning and winnowing of the freshly harvested crops in the following April-May.

"The work of plowing and sowing was carried on simultaneously by means of a seeder – that is, a plow with an attachment that carried the seed from a container through a narrow funnel down to the furrow. The farmer was instructed to plow eight furrows to each strip of approximately twenty feet. He was told to see to it that the seed was placed at an even depth. Following the sowing, the furrows had to be cleared of clods, so that the sprouting of the barely would not be impeded. Instructions were also given for the proper harvesting, threshing and winnowing of grains."

Other inscribed clay tablets of the same period (about 3,500 years ago) speak of planting vegetable gardens and how they should be arranged and laid out. Natural insect and weed control measures are given, too. Kramer also noted that "one of the more significant horticultural techniques practiced in Sumer from the earliest days was shade-tree gardening–that is, the planting of broad shade trees to protect the garden plants from sun and wind; an entire chapter is devoted to this subject alone in his very readable book.

Henri Frankfort mentioned in *The Birth of Civilization In The Near East* (London: Williams and Norgate Ltd., 1954; p.39) one exceptional aspect to Sumerian agriculture, that of "fine stock-breeding," which he described as being quite "innovative." And V. Gordon Childe in *Man Makes Himself* (Oxford: Oxford University Press, 1939; pp. 87-90) offers an attractive hypothesis that the origins for such a science may have originated before the Flood.

The archaeological evidence from Sumer also suggests other marvelous inventions, such as wheeled vehicles (both four- and two-wheelers), superb metalworks of gold, silver, copper, and bronze, some iron machinery and tools, and, most intriguing of all, asphalt. M.A. Littauer's and J. H. Crouwel's *Wheeled Vehicles and Ridden Animals In The Ancient Near East* (Leiden/Koln: E.J. Brill, 1979) and Andre Parrot's *Sumer* (New York: Golden Press, 1961) are worth reading sometime to expand your own knowledge about Sumerian wheeled vehicles, metalwork, and ironwork. On the top of one of the stone boxes which Brewer and I retrieved from the old Jaredite cave, there is a raised figure decoration of a man riding a two-wheeled chariot drawn by a single horse. This representation from around 750 B.C. closely parallels some of the Sumerian two-wheeled vehicles of a much earlier period and also demonstrates that the wheel was known in ancient America, contrary to the oft-repeated denials of many prejudiced archaeologists.

In the time of the Great Tower, asphalt was in common use for things such as road making, roofing and waterproofing. According to Henry Frederick Lutz's translation of *Sumerian Temple Records of The Late Ur Dynasty* (Berkley, CA: University of California Press, 1928; Univ. of Calif. Pubs. in Semitic Philology 9(2):167), asphalt was a frequent part of temple inventories at the time. And The Septuagint Version of The Old Testament and Aporypha (London: Samuel Bagster & Sons, 1851; p. 12, Chapt. 11, Verse 4) informs us that "the brick was to them for stone, and their mortar was bitumen," during the construction of the Tower itself. Perhaps that's why one third of it burned so well when the Lord struck it with lightning, while a great earthquake

Decorated stone box and lid top with raised figures from the Jaredite cave high in the mountains near Manti, Ut. Notice especially the half-figure of a man in a two-wheeled chariot holding on to the reins of the horse drawing it. Such pictorial evidence is offered as proof that ancient Americans had access to wheeled vehicles in spite of an opposing view supported by many archaeologists.

took down another third of it, leaving just a mere third standing in rubble (see Jasher 9:38).

It isn't unreasonable to assume that Jared and his brother Mahonri Moriancumer and those who went with them across the inland seas of Asia to the coasts of China, took along some of this same bitumen with them to use in their own barges that God inspired them to make with which to cross the mighty oceans. We know for sure that Noah used it extensively when he built the ark in South Carolina (as mentioned in the previous chapter). In the rare, out-of-print archaeological magazine called *Records of The Past* (1(12):363-380; December 1902), George Smith presented some new data about Noah that had come from several cuneiform tablets found in the ancient palace library of King Assurbanipal of Nineveh around 660 B.C.

We learn from these clay documents that the ark was at least as tall as a six-story building. Noah divided "it into seven compartments; [and] its floors [were] divided into nine chambers each." It also contained a short mast and rudder pole with which to give the huge vessel better steering capabilities. Noah gave the ship a trial launch but soon discovered it leaking like a sieve in a number of places. So he, his sons and their assorted servant laborers took buckets of bitumen and coated everything inside and out with several layers of this black gooey stuff; they followed it up with a hard shellac covering for good measure. Included with all of their personal effects and belongings inside the ark were vast amounts of "collected silver and gold," which undoubtedly helped to restart a new world economy after the Flood.

From a very old Arabic manuscript found in the library of the Convent of St. Catherine on Mount Sinai comes a rather interesting account of some of the "particulars as to the internal arrangements of the ark and the distribution of [its] passengers. The beasts and cattle were battened down in the main hold; the middle deck was occupied by birds; and the promenade deck was reserved for Noah and his family. But the men and the women were kept strictly apart. The patriarch and his sons lodged in the east end of the ark, and his wife and his sons' wives lodged in the west end" (see James George Frazer's *Folk-Lore In The Old Testament* (London: Macmillan & Co., Ltd., 1918; I:145-46). We don't know if similar arrangements were followed by the Jaredites when they built and launched their eight barges off the Shandong Peninsula in eastern China, but if separation between the sexes in public meetings and long journeys was customary, then the same thing would surely apply with them.

Returning to Smith's translation of those Chaldean Deluge tales from Nineveh, we find the ark resting down in a high mountain valley near the top of Ararat, with a portion of one end partly submerged in a newly-formed lake. (Before this there were no lakes or streams, but when the waters receded, it left lakes in the hollows of the mountains and streams began to run from them. See *Memoirs of The American Folklore Society* 6:20; 1898.) The occupants left the ark and Noah built a stone altar upon which he burned dried reeds, pine needles, simgar, calamus, cedar and several other aromatic herbs. A sacrifice of gratitude was then offered up unto God for His safety and protection in getting them through the worst crisis of their lives. Noah suffered from some form of skin disease at the time (probably eczema, psoriasis or shingles due to extreme stress from the Flood's awful impact); he was instructed to go and dip himself in the waters of this new glacial lake, which he did, and got well again. According to Chaldean, Babylonian, and Greek myths found on those Nineveh documents, Noah never died but was promptly translated to heaven after his mortal ministry had ended. That heaven, however, was undoubtedly Enoch's City which then still hovered in the lower reaches of the earth's atmosphere, where he joined his relative Enoch. An LDS footnote to the foregoing: Joseph Smith identified Noah as Gabriel who appeared to Zacharias and to Mary to announce the births of John the Baptist and Jesus Christ; he also mentioned that Elias was another title by which Noah is sometimes known (see *Teachings of The Prophet Joseph Smith* SLC: Deseret News Press, 1938; p. 157; and Doctrine & Covenants 27:6-7).

A final look at the ark from someone who actually visited it when he was a child, shows us something about the fabulous technology that was carried over from the Flood and later applied towards erecting the Great Tower. My informant was a Kurdish refugee named Mustafa, age 63, from northwestern Iraq. I met him while doing stake missionary work one time and arranged through an English-speaking relative of his to return the next day for an interview.

Sometime in the early to mid-1940's when Mustafa was only ten years old, he and his grandfather ascended Ararat in search of a few lost sheep. They took their time and slowly made their way up the side of the mountain. He said it seemed like a few hours of climbing before they found two of the strays; his grandfather agreed to take the pair back to their base camp at the bottom while he continued searching for the remaining one. Being nimble-footed, of light weight and energetic, he was able to negotiate some of the cliffs on the lower part of the mountain "like a mountain goat" (to use his own description).

On coming down the other side, he noticed a small, clear blue lake in the distance with something partly sticking out of the water over near the shady side where a portion of a frozen glacier could be seen. He recalled the breathless excitement he felt as a boy while carefully making his way around the perimeter of the lake towards this large object. What a queer boat, he thought to himself, as he came within closer range of it. It looked to him like a very long and narrow barge with a flat nose and a flat bottom. The very top, however, was rounded like a cigar with only a small walkway just a few feet wide going down the center from end to end. It had stubby masts where he surmised sails must have once been.

Upon reaching this strange vessel, he ran his hand over some of the wood and discovered it to be hard like stone (or petrified). He walked around to the one end sticking out of the water and noticed that it had been somewhat dismantled. He carefully crept inside where the temperature turned chilly and looked around. He noticed that it contained numerous small rooms and some big ones, too, with very high ceilings that were framed in with massive timbers he judged to have been one yard in width. He imagined they must have held very tall animals much bigger in size than conventional elephants.

Some of the rooms were lined with tiers of cages made from rough-hewn, thin slats on the sides, top and bottom; but the front portions of each had what appeared to be tiny rows of iron rebar similar to what is used in cement work for building foundations, only not quite as thick. All of the ironwork was heavily encrusted with thick layers of rust. He assumed this must have been where poultry was once kept.

One unusual feature he would never forget, he claimed, was the thick, shiny, almost waxy paint that covered both the interior as well as the exterior. There were numerous window holes in the top just under an overhanging roof. He couldn't begin to guess the measurements of them except to say that they were ingeniously constructed, each one having its own little door with an iron ring attached at the bottom, through which was run some kind of cable that had once been attached to pulleys to either end of the vessel. This must have been operated by some kind of spring mechanism that allowed these portal doors to be opened and closed together at random from the front or the back.

Mustafa said that everything about this enormous vessel was simply grand. And that it bore all the earmarks of having been made by a highly-advanced civilization of some kind. He was there all alone in the stillness and solitude of this curiously-made craft. But he never once felt frightened nor alarmed. It was almost like standing in a mosque on prayer day by yourself, he claimed (Mustafa is Islamic). He left that place in total awe and with a wonderfully prickly sensation he felt all over his skin. Many more hours passed, but with the aid of a full moon he eventually made his way out of this well-hidden valley with its famously secreted relic and down the other side, where he met his very anxious father near the break of day. He related everything he had seen and his grandfather believed him, but told him to use wisdom in whom he chose to share it with.

Here the story abruptly ended. I watched Mustafa carefully with discerning eyes, as he arose out of his chair, shook my hand, gave his head a slight bowing nod, and was off into the other room to get something to eat. There were no pretensions about this man and he had related everything in a very sober, matter-of-fact way, just as if it had happened to him yesterday. His vivid recollection of small details when combined with a humble demeanor, convinced me that his adventure was genuine. Not only that, but the spirit or vibratory influence which emanated from his unassuming being left a calming presence with me. No dishonest person or teller of tall tales could ever have such a peaceful tranquility around himself or herself for very long.

CHAPTER TEN

CURIOUS INSIGHTS INTO CAIN, CITY OF ENOCH, AND THE GREAT TOWER OF BABEL

The reader may be wondering about now why there have been so many references made in the text to people and events on both sides of the Flood. The necessity for this is quite easy to understand: One cannot appreciate the very high levels of technological and sociological advancements of the Jaredite civilization, which reigned supreme over the entire Western Hemisphere for almost two millenniums, without casting some attention to the antediluvian world itself. The culture before the Flood contributed significantly to the new culture after the Flood. And the Jaredites were right in the middle of this exploding knowledge and rapidly growing technology. Looking at it another way, we can draw distinct parallels between the archaeologically verifiable Olmec culture that sprouted up in the tropical lowlands of the Mexican states of Veracruz and Tabasco and the scripturally supported Jaredite empire that sprang up a little further to the south in the Yucatan Peninsula. Both were contemporaries of each other, coming into existence at about the same time. Michael Coe, an anthropologist from Yale University who has extensively studied the Olmec, has used superlatives such as "extraordinary vitality," "overwhelmingly beautiful," and "inspiring creativity" to try and adequately describe in his book *America's First Civilization* (New York: American Heritage Publishing Co., 1968; p. 127) the sheer force of technological and cultural genius that went into the making of this mighty society. Well, from what the Book of Mormon tells us about the Jaredites, they were certainly not one whit behind the Olmecs for the simple reason that both cultures are one and the same!

Now the Book of Ether, which is an abbreviated history of the people from the Tower of Babel, mentions the following foundry activities of these ancient Jaredites (11:23): "And they did work in all manner of ore, and they did make gold, and silver, and iron, and brass, and all manner of metals; and they did dig it out of the earth; wherefore they did cast up mighty heaps of earth to get ore, of gold, and of silver, and of iron, and of copper. And they did work all manner of fine work." Brigham Young mentions in his personal history (see *Millennial Star* 26(33):520; August 13, 1864) of himself and others regularly discovering some of these ancient iron objects in the routine plowing of their fields in different communities all over upstate New York: "From the time father Bosley located near Avon he found and ploughed up axes and irons, and had sufficient to make his mill irons, and had always abundance of iron on hand without purchasing [any]. In the towns of Bloomfield, Victor, Manchester, and in the regions round about, there were hills [in] which were frequently found [numerous iron objects]. It was a common occurrence in the country [at the time] to plough up axes, which I have done many times myself."

Well, there were certainly plenty of ironworks to be found on the plains of Shinar when Jared, his brother and their people were counted among the 600,000 or so laborers who worked through blood, sweat, and tears to build that mighty edifice for King Nimrod's pleasure. For without iron tools, the Great Tower to Heaven could never have been constructed; more than likely it would have turned out to be a miserable heap sinking to Hell without the benefit of iron. And yet to dramatize the lengthy existence of iron, we are forced, out of necessity, to turn back to the antediluvian era to show that such a metallurgical science has always been around since the very beginning of time itself.

To do so, we must go back to Cain for the umpteenth time and his own wicked use of iron in two different ways. Arnauld D'Andilly's French translation of *The Works of Josephus* (already cited in the previous chapter) observed that Cain and Abel "were of very different inclinations. Abel the younger honored justice and (supposing God was present in all his actions) he always and wholly fixed his thoughts on virtue. But Cain (being a wicked man, and addicted to unsatiable desire of profit) was he that first found out the use of the plough." In other words, Abel was a virtuous man but Cain was a greedy capitalist, which caused God to accept the former's offering but to reject the latter's oblations. This infuriated Cain and he soon blamed his brother for the negative outcome. According to the Syriac version of Genesis

4:1-16, both brothers became embroiled in a fierce argument with deadly consequences for each of them.

The Vetus Testamentum (26(1):76), an international quarterly journal published for the study of the Old Testament, recorded highlights of their nasty embranglement: "And when they had gone out to the field, Cain spoke and said to Abel, 'I know that the world was not created through mercy, and that it is not governed according to the fruit of good deeds, and that there is a favoritism in judgment. That is why your offering was accepted with favor whereas my offering was not accepted from me with favor.' Abel replied and said to Cain, 'I know that the world was created through mercy, and is governed according to the fruit of good deeds. Since my offering was better than yours, my offering was accepted from me with favor whereas your offering was not accepted from you with favor.' Cain replied and said to Abel, 'There is no judgment and there is no Judge. There is no other world, nor is there the giving of good reward to the righteous nor punishment of the wicked.' And Abel replied and said to Cain, 'There is judgment and there is a Judge. There is another world, and there is the giving of good reward to the righteous and punishment of the wicked in the world-to-come.' On account of this issue they were arguing in the field, and Cain arose against Abel his brother, and he slew him." The apocryphal Book of Jasher (1:25) informs us of the manner in which this murder was accomplished: "And Cain hastened and rose up, and took the iron part of his ploughing instrument, with which he suddenly smote his brother and he slew him and Cain spilt the blood of his brother Abel upon the earth, and the blood of Abel streamed upon the earth before the flock." And the Prophet Joseph Smith identified the precise whereabouts that this sad tragedy occurred–"Far West [Caldwell County, Missouri] was the spot where Cain killed Abel" (see *The Reed Peck Manuscript* (Salt Lake City: Utah Lighthouse Ministry; p. 5.) The pseudepigraphal work *Life of Adam and Eve* suggests that after committing this heinous crime on Abel, Cain added further insult to injury by scooping up some of Abel's spilled blood with a cupped hand and drank it in the mistaken belief that he could inherit some of his brother's noble virtues (see James H. Charlesworth's *The Old Testament Pseudepigrapha* (Garden City, NY; Doubleday & Co., Inc., 1985; 2:267).

Nothing more was heard of Cain after he jumped off the roof of the ark and wandered away. But the technical know-how for making iron plows similar to the one used to slay Abel, was carried into the ark by Noah and his sons. When they disembarked on Ararat and went down to settle on the extremely fertile plains below, an obviously brisk business in plow manufacturing began. Such ironworks which expanded their operations include many other useful tools and pieces of equipment, not to mention, unfortunately, weapons of war such as swords, daggers, and spears. Eventually came wheeled carts, wagons, and chariots with their iron spokes, rims, and axles.

But the painful lessons of the recent Deluge soon faded from people's memories and it wasn't long before the wicked were in "business as usual," according to The Book of Jasher (7:44-47). "And Nimrod dwelt in Shinar, and he reigned securely, and he fought with his enemies and he subdued them, and he prospered in all his battles, and his kingdom became very great. And all nations and tongues heard of his fame, and they gathered themselves to him, and they bowed down to the earth, and they brought him offerings, and he became their lord and king. And they all dwelt with him in the city of Shinar, and Nimrod reigned in the earth over all the sons of Noah, and they were all under his power and counsel. And all the earth was of one tongue and words of union. But Nimrod did not go in the ways of the Lord. And he was more wicked than all the men that were before him, from the days of the Flood until those days." Nimrod had great physical strength and remarkable intuitive powers on account of the priesthood garments made from animal skins that Adam had worn in his time. They were made by God for Adam, who surrendered them to Enoch, who gave them to Methuselah when he was translated to heaven with his entire city; at the death of Methuselah, Noah acquired them "and brought them to the ark, and they were with him until he went out of the ark." But then his adopted son or the one by another wife, namely Ham, stole them away "and hid them from his brothers" and father. Ham's firstborn son Cush received them upon reaching manhood and he "also concealed them from his sons and brothers," finally giving them to his son Nimrod "when he was twenty years old" (see Jasher 7:24-30).

Now at that time, the massive chunk of earth taken up from where the Gulf of Mexico now resides and called the City of Enoch, hovered overhead some seventy miles in the lower parts of our planet's atmosphere (see the published version of Wilford Woodruff's Journal 7:129 under the entry for March 30th, 1873). An earlier Church President, Brigham Young claimed that "the City of Enoch was caught up a little ways from the earth, and that the city was within the first sphere above the earth. And [Nimrod and his people imagined] that if they could get a tower high enough, they might get to heaven, where the City of Enoch and the inhabitants thereof were located. So they went to work and built a tower" (see *Journal of Discourses* 16:50). But Woodruff and Young both got their ideas from that great earthly fountainhead of eternal knowledge, the Prophet Joseph Smith himself. According to the *Nauvoo Journal of George Laub* (BYU Studies 18(2):175;Winter 1978), Joseph gave a discourse on April 13, 1843 in which he stated: "Now I will tell [you] the designs of building the tower of Babel. It was designed to go to the city of Enoch, for the veil was not so thick that it hid it from their sight. So they concluded to go to the city of Enoch, for God gave him place above this impure earth." Apostle Orson F. Whitney rightly called the construction of this Great Tower to that suspended city in the atmosphere, "the mightiest engineering feat" ever accomplished, involving very "cunning skills" (see *Deseret News Weekly* 40(2):75; January 4th, 1890).

Elder Whitney also ventured where few preachers have dared to go when he gave a brutally honest analysis of how that orb got where it did. "How was this miracle of Enoch's city accomplished? Not by an empty and vain profession of righteousness; not by men seeking themselves, and their own honor and glory. Not by heaping up gold and silver and precious stones. Not by the rich grinding under heel the poor; not by the proud despising the humble. And not by the poor hating and envying the rich. It was not done by loving the things of this world. But it was by the practice of the grand principle of self denial—the principle of sacrifice—the foundation stone of the great fabric of human salvation. Zion of old, attaching herself to these grand principles, became so pure, so sanctified, that she could no longer dwell amid the surroundings of this fallen world. She had to leave Babylon behind her; to be loosed from the earth just as a boat is loosed from the dock where it has been fastened, to sail away with the current that carries it on. That current was the current of progress, of advancement in the highest of all civilizations, a spiritual civilization, which alone can redeem us from our present weak and fallen condition."

In fact much of Elder Whitney's talk was devoted to the translated Enoch, his city in the clouds, and the Tower itself. It was so good that after giving it in his own 18th Ward on Sunday, September 22nd, 1889, he was asked by the First Presidency of the Church to give it to all other wards in the Salt Lake Valley as well as a number of others in outlying towns throughout the Utah Territory. At age 22 he had an open vision of the Savior in Gethsemane in which the Lord implied that young Whitney would eventually be called as an Apostle of His someday (this occurred on April 9, 1906); a year later, at age 23, he was called to be a ward bishop while still "an unmarried youth."

But it is with family patriarchal blessings that we learn about his remarkable lineages going back to the Tower of Babel. His grandfather Newel K. Whitney, who was the second Presiding Bishop of the Church, was told in a patriarchal blessing given to him by Patriarch Joseph Smith, Sr. on September 14th, 1835 in Kirtland, Ohio that he was a direct lineal "descendant of Melchizedek" or Shem (one of Noah's sons), and that one of his upcoming posterity would "be like unto [Melchizedek] before the Lord." It was probably for these reasons that Father Smith described him as being "a strange man in thy ways" and "not like the ways of other men."

Orson Ferguson Whitney had eight separate patriarchal blessings himself spanning a period of 41 years (1879-1920). Patriarch O. N. Liljenquist told by inspiration on February 26th, 1879 that he would "have faith like unto the brother of Jared" and have the same kind of priesthood which the former did "to perform many marvelous and mighty works." In October, 1881, he received two more patriarchal blessings within less than a week: William J. Smith blessed him with "the faith and power of Enoch of old [who] caused the earth to shake at his words;" and Abraham O. Smoot promised him a "Spiritual quickening" of his mortal body like unto what Enoch experienced, if he desired to live to see Christ come in the Millennium (apparently he didn't want this and passed away at age 75). Smoot also told him that he would "have power to command the elements, if necessary" like those of old; and that "the spirits that have gone hence [shall] visit and revisit thee." This was fulfilled many times over, but particularly with regard to some of those who lived at the time of the Great Tower. (See Orson F. Whitney's autobiography, *Through Memory's Halls* (Independence, MO: Zion's Printing & Publishing Co., 1930; pp. 82-

83;106-107;16;411-414 in regard to the foregoing in the last two paragraphs.)

My father Jacob Heinerman, when but a youth of sixteen, attended what back then was referred to as a Cottage Meeting with other Aaronic Priesthood members his own age in the home of a ward priesthood leader. This was about 1930. The purpose of such Cottage Meetings was to promote better activity and more frequent attendance among Aaronic youth, a number of whom usually became inactive during their teenage years. Such group meetings served as working and social units in which young men participated in gospel discussions monitored by an adult advisor, heard speeches from invited guests, saw church-produced filmstrips sometimes, and occasionally engaged in social events.

At this particular gathering which my father attended, Apostle Whitney happened to be the unannounced speaker. He related some events connected with pioneer days and spoke briefly about the contents made in a couple of these blessings by different stake patriarchs—that he would be visited by some of those behind the Veil. The question was put to him by one curious boy as to the identity of them. My father distinctly remembers Elder Whitney pausing to carefully ponder the question before giving an answer. He finally replied that at one time in the night Noah and Melchizedek appeared to him with information concerning his own direct lineage back to them and the significance of this in his own mortal ministry. This fulfilled, he noted, what Patriarch William J. Smith had pronounced upon his head in a blessing given to him on April 19th, 1891, a small portion of which he then read: "The visions of eternity shall be continually unfolded to thy view."

Another inquisitive lad wanted to know "what else they said." Elder Whitney smiled with some patient benevolence, my father stated, and then quietly remarked that his visitors had told him that the foundation base of the Tower of Babel would have filled up most of what then constituted the geographical boundaries of Salt Lake City. There were a number of 'oohs' and 'ahhs' heard from the surprised youngsters following his statement. (It may be noteworthy here to relate, according to the apocryphal Book of Jasher 9:38 that it took a man "three days' walk" to completely go around the Tower, obviously showing its enormous circumference.)

Elder Whitney wasn't the only church member privileged to learn things about the Great Tower on the plains of Shinar. In one of the serial publications of the Daughters of the Utah Pioneers, *Our Pioneer Heritage* (Salt Lake City: Utah Printing Co., 1963; 6:357) is mentioned the experience of William Decatur Kartchner, taken from his own journal: "December 7, 1882. I was sick with biliousness and sinking spells and was unconscious. I had prayed to know if my labors had been accepted and was immediately made whole. Such joy I had never experienced before. And on the night of March 19th, 1883 was taken with a sinking spell and was unconscious part of the evening. I fear to die with a great fear. I saw a vision of the Tower of Babel. Its center and foundation were solid with brick and lime, with a winding stairway. I saw the Brother of Jared and company travel marks to the seaside and the beautiful mount of white and transparent rock that the brother of Jared asked the Lord to touch, that they might shine forth in the barges while crossing the sea. I saw the place of landing. It resembled a valley I had seen in a former vision. The gold they found for making the plates on which the [Book of Ether] was made."

Similar experiences were connected with the building of the Idaho Falls Temple, which was dedicated in Idaho Falls, ID by Church President George Albert Smith on Sunday, September 23, 1945 at 10 a.m. While murals in the World Room, Garden of Eden room, and Creation Room had been done before the dedication, murals for the Celestial Room were not completed until 1949 by famed LDS artist Lee Greene Richards. According to one informant: "They were painted on several large canvasses in Salt Lake and then shipped to Idaho Falls. The artist, though very ill at the time, accompanied them and directed their placement in the Celestial Room from a bed made there. A crew of six to eight men fastened them carefully to the walls with white lead, then covered the seams." The artist, who was related to pioneer Apostle Willard Richards, died in February 1950. An editorial in the Church-owned newspaper, The *Deseret News* (February 22, 1950) noted that he was one of the most "widely acclaimed landscape artists and painter of portraits" in the country. "His artwork began as a mere child, and continued up until a few days before his death." *The Journal History of the Church*, under the date of February 23rd, 1950 (p. 2) mentioned him "growing up with a group of young artists who became known as the 20th Ward group and included such noted men as

Mahonri Young, Alma B. Wright, Jack Sears, George M. Ottinger, Alfred Lambourne and H. L. A. Culmer."

One who knew his talents well claimed that "Brother Richards' talent is really a spiritual gift, in that he often paints what he has seen in dreams or visions." That was apparently the case with his most intriguing mural, then located "on the southerly part of the west wall" of the Celestial Room in the Idaho Falls Temple. It inspired more comments from Latter-day Saints gathering in and passing through this room than any other temple mural. (When the temple was closed down for a year of extensive remodeling, from September 1972 till October 1973, it was removed and a less inspiring mural substituted in its place.)

The original mural "showed heavenly buildings" suggesting "a holy city...coming down out of heaven." One of the later temple presidents explained to some of the temple workers, while they stood in front of this marvelous mural, that "it was the City of Enoch and the righteous people with him." When someone once asked Lee Richards how he happened to come by way of that particular scene, the artist explained that it had come to him in a vision one time and remained present long enough for him to capture enough of the details of it. Later, when the First Presidency commissioned him to do some murals for the Celestial Room, the inspiration came to him to paint the scene from the vision of Enoch's City. (Information for the foregoing, unless otherwise noted within the text came from several different sources: Delbert V. Groberg, *The Idaho Falls Temple* (Salt Lake City: Publishers Press, 1985; pp. 123-24;237); Blanche Humphreys, *Friday Nights LDS Sociables* (Idaho Falls, 1980; p. 15 "Idaho Falls Temple"); and an oral interview with Arthur Moregenegg, Sunday, January 25, 1970 in the Idaho Falls 4th Ward; he spoke with the artist in the temple at the time his murals were being installed.)

Another church member who had his own special witness of ancient things was a kind, humble soul named Dorris Durrell Leavitt. At the time of his birth on April 3, 1914 in Idaho Falls, the medical doctor who was then delivering him became impatient because things were going slower than he wanted them to. Grabbing a pair of forceps, he reached inside Sister Leavitt's birth canal, seized the newborn's head and gave a mighty tug to bring the child out more quickly. As a result of his hastiness, Dorris remained paraplegic for the remainder of his life (he died on Joseph Smith's birthday, December 23rd, 1982 in the rest home facility beside the LDS Hospital which then stood next to the temple grounds on the banks of the Snake River). He was also born with a cleft palate, which made speaking awkward and getting others to understand what he was trying to say even more frustrating at times.

I met this unique individual while residing in the Idaho Falls 4th Ward and working as a line cook at the Westbank Restaurant and Coffee Shop directly across the river from the hospital and temple grounds. I discovered upon becoming secretary of the Elders' Quorum, that Dorris was a member of our quorum. I went over to his simple abode, introduced myself and became acquainted with him. Over the next couple of years while I resided in that city, a wonderful friendship developed between both of us. He taught me the beauty and patience and perseverance which served me well in my later life; and I, in turn, did things for him around the house which he couldn't do very well himself. Still, he managed to get around pretty well on a little wooden wheeled cart which had been especially made for his particular needs. At first glance and without knowing the man, one would be mistakenly led to think that he was nothing but a crippled, drooling imbecile with a lunatic grin and eyeglasses thick enough to pass for binoculars. But in this case, the outward appearance could be very deceiving, for underneath lurked a very sharp mind and a highly intelligent spirit. Some of the deepest philosophical conversations that I ever had with anyone were spent in pleasant hours with this man. He was both a joy and an inspiration to know and be around.

The following incredible narrative is taken from one of my early journals under the date of Saturday, May 1st, 1971, just as I wrote it out from the scribbled notes I made of the marvelous things he told me when I visited him that afternoon for several hours.

"The thought came to me this afternoon to go over to see Dorris Leavitt. I was busy with other things and figured I'd do it tomorrow after church. But the thought grew stronger and the feeling so intense that I left off my other affairs and ambled on over to his place, which is just a few blocks from the basement apartment. I rent from Ron Wilford and his wife (he's a 2nd couns[elor] in my ward bishopric).

"Found old Dorris sitting on the porch, enjoying the cool of the early evening. He was watering his front lawn with the hose, but not much water was coming out and he couldn't figure out why. I pointed to his right cart wheel which was directly over on the hose impeding the water's flow. He grinned and asked me to push him off, which I did. I sat beside him and we chatted a few on nothing in particular. Said he was glad to see me again and I returned like sentiments.

"After a short spell, he turned to me and asked if I would like to hear something that happened to him back in the 1940s sometime just before the [Idaho Falls] Temple was dedicated. I said sure and he asked me to turn the water off and come inside the house with him. He told me to close the door behind me.

"He pushed himself on his little cart towards the kitchen. I sat on the old davenport in the front room and watched him as he opened his fridge door, took out a bottle of milk, drank some it of, and then offered me the rest. I declined saying that I didn't believe in sharing someone else's saliva. He roared with laughter and replaced the bottle. He then pushed his cart backwards into the living room with his feet and stopped a short distance in front of me. He pushed his glasses up the bridge of his nose with his gnarled right hand.

"I got up and said, 'here let me clean those things for you, it's a wonder you can see anyway.' I took them into the kitchen and ran them under the sink tap, then wiped them with my handkerchief and took them back and placed them on his nose again. He cried out with glee that things looked much clearer for him now.

"After this, we sat silent for a couple of minutes while Dorris tried to regain his composure. Then in his typical slow, halting fashion, he told me he was going to tell me a grand vision he had one day while sitting in that room looking out the window towards the temple. He said it was precious to him and that he had only shared it with his mother and a few others.

"I asked if it was all right to take notes and he nodded. I grabbed a folded brown paper Safeway shopping bag and held pen in hand as he started to talk. He said that his mother used to read to him, from the scriptures often when he was a boy. And that he loved to hear about events of the past. And had often wished in his heart as he grew older that he could have lived back then and met some of the characters he heard about.

"He said he had always been fascinated with the big tower built to reach heaven. He said it didn't seem that such a thing was humanly possible to do. He sometimes wondered about this, but didn't let his doubt interfere with his beliefs any. He couldn't remember the exact day or year or even how old he was when this vision happened. But he was sitting in front of one living room window (the one with the steamer trunk in front of it) one day sometime before the temple on Memorial Drive was finished. As he looked out in that direction, everything seemed to gradually change and the present scenery passed away and was replaced with another. He compared it to changing picture cards in a stereoscope—everything then just melted away and he saw instead of a temple, a big, big, building that seemed to fill the whole surrounding landscape.

"As the vision broadened out for him, he saw numerous people everywhere engaged in all types of useful activities. There must have been tens of thousands of campfires burning all around and a regular tent city had sprung up for as far as the eye could see. Some were making mud bricks. Others were baking them in firing ovens. Still others were busily applying a shiny waxlike substance to every brick made. Scores of men hauled loads and loads of brick up in a gigantic winding staircase. He saw huge beasts of burden the likes of which he'd never seen being used to move and haul heavy objects around. Others were occupied with metal making, banging on big chunks of red-hot iron with large flat-edged hammers. Dorris said he craned his neck so far to the left that it gave him a crick as he tried to get a better look at the tower itself from another angle. He said it was tall in the air—that he couldn't even see the top of it.

"The landscape was dominated by the biggest crowd he ever imagined possible—literally hundreds of thousands. He compared it with the crowds he'd seen on TV sometimes on New Year's Eve that gather in Times Square in New York to welcome in a brand new year. They were of that size. While gazing in awe on this busy scene of packed humanity, he was given to understand that what lay before him was the Tower of Babel and those involved in its erection. There then came to his mind a vivid recollection of the several times he had doubted of its actual existence. This made him feel very bad for having ever doubted the scriptures about such a thing.

"The scene shifted a little to the left and only a part of the tower remained visible. He then saw a large group of people living together in tents. Outside these tents they had staked by the back legs, with

The remarkably preserved remains of a Jaredite royal mummy (presumably a king) entombed in a stone sarcophagus in an ancient mountainous burial chamber in Sanpete County, Utah. This figure measured nine feet two inches tall. Note the decidedly proto-Mongoloid facial features which are typical of present-day Mongolians and other Oriental races. The hair and beard were a dull, rust-red color. Some of the original emigrants from the Tower, (including Jared and his brother and their extended families) may have looked this way. (Original sketch made by Earl John Brewer.)

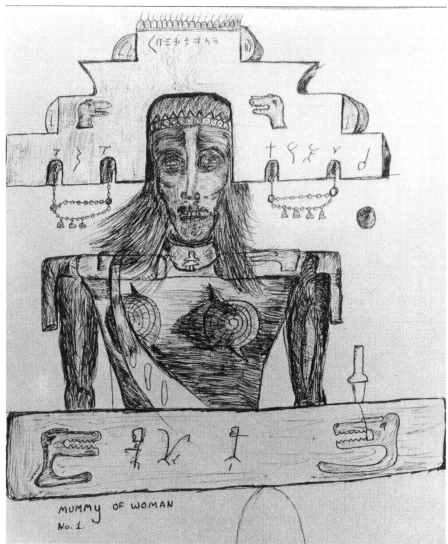

MUMMY OF WOMAN No. 1.

The wonderfully intact remains of a Jaredite royal mummy (presumably a queen) enshrined in a large stone coffin in an ancient treasure cave located between the small Mormon communities of Manti and Ephraim in southcentral Utah. This particular individual measured eight feet eight inches. Observe the enormous headdress and dragon markings, so typical for women of royalty in some of China's earliest dynasties. Strands of mud-brown and ugly gray were intermingled with mostly straw-colored hair, giving the appearance of being "dish water" blonde. Radiocarbon testing of some hair and nail clippings and tissue samples dated this and her male companion to between 800-700 B.C. Some Jaredite women who emigrated from the Tower of Babel with their husbands may have had similar features, including the tall height. (Original sketch made by Earl John Brewer.)

148

heavy chains, several tall hairy elephants that were as big as the old tree in his front yard there. He saw inside the tent and was given to understand that everyone there belonged to one family. He counted 17 people in all. One man who was taller than the rest and had a medium beard was explaining something to the rest of them. At that point, this portion of the vision became audible. The man was attempting to tell the others to not laugh so much, to remember God more and his promises to them. But everyone just ignored him except one man who came over and took his brother aside and told him that he believed in the things he was trying to teach the others.

"Doris said the language they spoke was foreign to him but that he could still understand what was being said by the Holy Spirit's interpretation of these things to him. He said that the identities of both men were made known to him then and that the believing one's name was Jared and the other man doing all the talking was his brother.

"Again the scene shifted and he saw these two men talking with some of their friends and a few believed in the words they spoke. He said that from one angle in this particular scene he could see in the distance the upper part of the tower and behind it the moon. Dorris was startled by this because he had always been taught by his mother that the moon was further away in space and was surprised to see it so close then, almost like you could reach up and touch it.

"Next there was brought before his view a long caravan of people with numerous beasts in their company. Not everyone looked the same, though – some had different shades of skin color, browns, yellows, reds, and whites all mixed up. This great company of people were then plodding through a wilderness that looked barren, not a tree or bush in sight anywhere.

"There stood in their way what looked like a big mountain range. The fellow Jared inquired of his brother to do something about it since it looked impassable. Dorris said the brother separated himself some distance from the rest of the group, got down on his knees and prostrated himself low on the ground with outstretched hands. It seemed like he was in the act of praying to God, but Dorris thought this was a strange way to do it. He was given to understand that this was the way men prayed back then. He said the brother called out in a loud voice to God and Dorris could understand some of his prayer in spite of the strange language spoken. He was bent down on his face for some time but was pleading that the mountain range in front of them would be removed. At that moment a great noise was heart and in the distance an enormous cloud of dust arose and covered everything. When things had settled down there was no longer any mountain standing in their way. Dorris said it had just collapsed and crumbled to rubble before his very eyes.

"From the wilderness the scenery moved to a seashore somewhere with an ocean view to it. Here everyone settled down and made themselves comfortable for awhile. The brother went off into a high mountain surrounded by thick clouds that gave off occasional flashes of lightning. He later returned with a knapsack containing a number of glass balls the size of goose eggs that illuminated in the dark. Dorris described the light as being soft like some fluorescent lights were, not harsh at all to the eyes. These were placed in different sailing vessels that were shaped like gigantic cigars and as long as tall trees.

"There seemed to be some sort of contention between a few of the people there. Not everyone wanted to go into those vessels. Some chose to stay behind being comfortable with the way things were. There was a separation of personal property for those who remained behind. Dorris saw the brother give a tearful embrace to one of his daughters who's husband didn't want to go along. A powerful wind arose in the waters and drove the vessels away from shore. They traveled for a great distance. Dorris said that they were sometimes tossed about in hurricane storms but soon struck land in another strange place.

"The final scene shown to him was everyone kneeling around a big stone altar on which some kind of animal was being sacrificed that Dorris had never seen before. The brother was performing the ritual while Jared stood off to one side with the others encircling the altar. He understood that it was being done out of appreciation for a safe trip they had across the waters. Dorris could hear and understand some of the words which the brother was offering up on bended knees with both arms raised high over his head.

"Dorris said after this point things gradually began to melt away and a cloudy image of the present landscape reappeared until everything was crystal clear to his view as it had been before. Here the glorious vision ended. By now Dorris had pulled his glasses off and with his good left hand was wiping away a stream of tears that poured out of his eyes. I too was visibly affected by all of this and bawled right along beside him for a couple of minutes.

"I got up, walked to Dorris and leaned over and kissed him on top of his bald head and thanked him for sharing this lovely experience with me. I returned to my apartment. in Wilford's basement and wrote out the entire account in my journal while it was still fresh in my mind and used my notes made on both sides of that shopping bag to fill in any missing pieces. It was after 1 a.m. that I finally turned in for the night but couldn't fall asleep yet. I just lay there in bed going over everything in my mind that he had told me and wondering whether or not I would ever live a good enough life to enjoy such things for myself someday.

"It was about then that the idea occurred to me as to why I had been so strongly prompted to visit Dorris Leavitt and also why the Lord had touched his heart enough to want to share such a sacred event with me. The idea came as both a thought and feeling together and was simply this–that someday I would become extensively involved with the culture of these people who came from the Tower and that this was the beginning of a process to adequately prepare me for that time to come. I reached over to my night stand, turned on the lamp and got up and went to my antique secretary desk. I sat down and entered the last few lines before calling it a night."

CHAPTER ELEVEN

IN SEARCH OF SAVANTS, SEERSTONES AND SANCTIFICATION

Rene Dubos, a world-renowned French-born American scientist, who discovered the first commercially produced antibiotic in 1939, wrote an international bestseller, *So Human an Animal* (New York: 1968; p.61) for which he won the Pulitzer Prize a year later. In his book was made this very significant statement: "Knowledge of the past is essential for the understanding of life in the present and in the future. Not because history repeats itself—which it never does exactly—but because the past is incorporated in all manifestations of the present and will thereby condition the future. At every stage, human life is the incarnation of the past."

The Jaredites were the original settlers of the Western Hemisphere. They came here before Columbus, the Vikings, and Mulekites, the Nephites and Lamanites, the Phoenicians, and anybody else. They were the first colonizers of the Americas after the Flood. Knowing something about their greatness and failures, and their triumphs and defeats will help us to perhaps better understand ourselves and where our own culture is headed unless we turn back to God and repent of all our sins. For in the mirror of past civilizations such as these people, we really see a true reflection of ourselves – all of our magnificent accomplishments are dwarfed in size by the many petty jealousies, vain ambitions, materialistic greed, carnal lusts and passions, and inconsiderate selfishness that are heaped upon our consciences like so many smelly dunghills, though we chose to ignore these messy parts of our putrid lives. After reigning supreme as the undisputed, sole occupants of the New World for almost 1,800 years, they ultimately perished in one of the worst civil wars that the earth has ever known.

On July 15th, 1860 in the crudely-erected Bowery on what

would eventually become Temple Square, President Brigham Young told a crowd of several thousand Saints in the sweltering sun: "Do you think there is calamity abroad now among the people? Not much. All that we have yet heard and all we have experienced is scarcely a preface to the sermon that is going to be preached with fire and sword, tempests, earthquakes, hail, rain, thunders and lightnings, and fearful destruction. You will hear of magnificent cities, now idolized by the people, sinking in the earth, entombing the inhabitants. The sea will heave itself beyond its bounds, engulfing mighty cities. Famine will spread over the nations, and nation will rise up against nation and states against states in our own country and in foreign lands. They will destroy each other, caring not for the blood and lives of their neighbors, or their families, or for their own lives. They will be like the Jaredites upon this continent, and will destroy each other to the last man, through the anger that the Devil will place in their hearts. They have rejected the words of life and are given over to Satan to do whatever he listeth to do with them" (see *Journal of Discourses* 8:123).

Apostle Orson Pratt preached a sermon in the Old Tabernacle on April 10th, 1870, in which he pinpointed the approximate landing site for the Jaredites when they reached the shores of the Americas: "They land[ed] a little south of the Gulf of Mexico, in the southwestern part of this north wing of our continent." He reminded his listeners of the warning which God gave to the Gentiles who presently occupy this hemisphere, that He would destroy them as He did those "brought from the Tower of Babel," if they didn't repent of their wicked ways. "What a difference our fathers, who lived forty years ago, and the present generation! Everyone can see it. The rising generations are proud, haughty, high-minded, lovers of pleasure more than lovers of God. I think the nation is pretty well ripened [in iniquity], and that it will not take much more to prepare them for the fulfillment of the[se] prophecies which I have been repeating. I do not know how long-suffering the Lord is. It is a good thing that He has wisdom, knowledge and understanding, that He is not a human being, or He would get wrathy and swallow up the people in a moment" (see *Journal of Discourses* 13:129;134;138). Hopefully, there still is enough time for us to learn from the mistakes of the Jaredites so that we can make the necessary adjustments in our own lives and culture before it comes too late to do so.

Those desiring a more thorough history of these people than what is offered here, are referred to that section known as the Book of Ether in The Book of Mormon. John Henry Evans, author of the popular work, *Joseph Smith, An American Prophet* (New York: The Macmillan Co., 1933; pp. 41-42) wrote the following words about this stirring epic: "The spectacular rise and fall of this mighty nation is covered in 32 pages of narrative that fairly sweeps one off one's feet." But this cannot be done by mere secular learning alone. For as Apostle John Taylor noted in an editorial he wrote for the *Times and Seasons* (5(23):747; December 15, 1844), which he once edited in Nauvoo, IL, "a little revelation [is needed] to unravel" the Jaredite history.

Now, a word or two about those illuminating stones brought down from Mount Shalem by Mahonri Moriancumer after the spiritual finger of the Lord had touched each of them at his request (see Ether 3:6). For unenlightened Gentiles and weak-in-the-faith Mormons, Ether's account about those sixteen glass stones touched by the finger of God and thereafter acting as substitute candles in the dark, has been ridiculed and treated as an absurd thing. Now, however, modern science has come along with some interesting technology that may help us to better appreciate this strange illumination phenomenon related in The Book of Mormon.

Sandia National Laboratories (SNL) shares research facilities in Albuquerque, New Mexico with the Department of Energy. Both have expended considerable funds and a great deal of effort in the creation of what some have termed "next generation" technology (meaning things that may someday prove useful in helping the present generation when they grow up). One such strange new invention is radioluminescent lights that can be used when no electrical power is available. These lights are made from a highly porous silica matrix called "aerogel" in which a phosphor such as zinc sulfide is dispersed.

A F.A.R.M.S. Update (#83) for July, 1992 explained how the illumination process unfolds. "The radioactive source of the lights is tritium gas, which when incorporated into the aerogel, actually becomes chemically bonded to the aerogel matrix. The radioactivity of tritium results in beta decay. The beta particles (electrons) permeate through the open spaces of the aerogel and stroke the phosphor particles, exciting them and causing them to emit light. The majority of the light emitted escapes to the outside, whereas the beta radiation is contained inside the matrix. Therefore, there is no appreciable external radiation."

The F.A.R.M.S. (Foundation for Ancient Research & Mormon Studies) article speculates "that the Jaredite stones were created in a similar fashion, according to existing physical laws. It is conceivable that the Lord could have altered some other molecule in the stone to create the radioactive isotope that would produce the glowing effect. It is also possible that He could have simply infused the stones with tritium gas as the Sandia researchers have done." As a side note, Spencer W. Kimball, while still an apostle, hinted at some nuclear element such as radium which the Lord may have put into those "molten small stones" that were "white and clear" (*Ensign*, April 1963, pp. 63-64).

The problem with the F.A.R.M.S. article, though, is that it looks at a spiritually-generated procedure from an entirely secular point of view. No one has ever considered the priesthood virtue emanating from our Lord constantly as being the TRUE SOURCE for the stones' continuous illumination. Now this virtue is an interesting thing to explore, for it sheds a great deal of understanding on how light came to be in otherwise dull rocks. The Prophet Joseph Smith, who felt it often in his own life, referred to this peculiar virtue of the priesthood as "the spirit of life." It would leave while blessing little children sometimes; and a small portion of it certainly left our Lord when the woman with the bloody issue touched the hem of Jesus' garment and was promptly made whole again (see Edwin F. Parry's *Joseph Smith's Teachings* (SLC: Deseret News, 1919; 155).

Ephraim K. Hanks, an early Mormon frontiersman and pioneer scout, was given the gift of healing upon joining the Church as a young man, which remained with him for the duration of his life on account of the tremendous virtue he carried within his being. Hundreds upon hundreds of sick Latter-day Saints with every imaginable disease known to man, were healed almost instantaneously under his capable administration. Richard K. Hanks' master's thesis on *Ephraim Hanks, Pioneer Scout* (Provo: BYU, 1973) makes reference to the priesthood virtue which emanated from his hands quite frequently and could actually be felt going into the bodies of those whom he was administering to at the time. Once, while serving as a stake patriarch, Hanks told an assembled congregation that the way for a priesthood holder to constantly maintain this virtue within himself was to "pray always, live a virtuous life, harbor compassion for the poor and down-trodden, and keep your attention always centered on the things of God." One of his grandsons, Verd Hanks, seems to have inherited the same principal, because every time he would administer to the sick "he said that he felt the virtue go out of him [and] into them" (see E. K. Hanks' *Wings of Faith* (1969;p. 20).

This priesthood virtue is imparted almost instantaneously from those filled with it unto others who are in dire need of the same. Apostle Heber C. Kimball had it to an amazing degree throughout his life. In a public sermon given once on Temple Square but only reported in the *New York Daily Tribune* (Friday, November 10th, 1865, p. 8, column 1) he recalled this from his early mission years to England: "I first baptized two sick women. They had to be carried in beds from the carriages to the water. The doctors had given them up. But when I baptized them, both recovered, from that hour. One was brother George Watt's mother; the other was Sister Wormsley. Many was healed by touching the hem of my garments. I did not know it then, but they was." And pioneer Samuel W. Richards recorded this in his journal under the date of Sunday, March 16th, 1856: "At the morning meeting in the Tabernacle, Elder Vernon preached bearing testimony of the truth. And relating his experience of the virtue imparted to him by Bro. Kimball when he put his hands upon his shoulders one time when going out of the Tabernacle" (see typescript copy of the *Journal of Samuel W. Richards* in Special Collections at the Lee Library at BYU in Provo under the date given above).

The virtue of the holy priesthood has been described in different ways by those who've felt it surging through their own bodily systems on various occasions. His autobiography, *Through Memory's Halls* (p. 87), Apostle Orson F. Whitney mentioned it "ran like liquid flame to the very tips of my fingers," while in the act of administering to a sick sister, who was instantly healed the moment it surged into her own body from his. Church President Wilford Woodruff felt this power often while serving as an apostle: One time he described it "like fire shut up in my bones" and on another occasion as being "full of that electric[al] fluid [that] felt as though I was on fire" (see Wilford Woodruff's Journal 1:524 under October 2nd, 1840; and 4:306 under February 18th, 1855). A more interesting description of this identical virtue emanating from celestialized beings, who visited one good Saint and imparted some of this divine substance to that fortunate individual, may be found in the *Woman's Exponent* (3:139; February 15th, 1875). Full details of this grand vision aren't necessary, save to say that in the middle of the night sometime a glorified but unmarried man and woman from the Celestial Kingdom, visited an unidentified Church member (thought to have been a female) the evening and morning of February 21st and 22nd, 1867 in her bedroom.

The following lines are excerpts from her lengthy account: "I woke up with a shock like lightning to my whole system, far more powerful than anything I had yet experienced. The room was filled with consuming flames, as a rushing, mighty wind, and a pillar of fire far above the brightness of the noonday sun, shining with clear, transparent brilliancy, lit upon me. As I gazed mute and helpless toward heaven, in the midst of the light, just beneath the ceiling, I saw two immortal beings. I saw that the light was centered immediately around their persons. So great was the power of God upon me [that] I had to sit still all the [next] afternoon, for I was still consumed as in a pillar of fire. And I felt so light in body for a week after, that I was half unconscious whether or not my feet touched the earth in walking."

In *Voices From The Past* (Provo: BYU, 1980; pp. 42-43) is recounted an incredible conversion experience by Francis Asbury Hammond, who knelt in prayer to know if the Book of Mormon was true or not. "I used but a very few words in my petition. Yet before the words were fairly uttered from my lips, a sheet of flame or fire commenced to descend upon me. Not very warm at first, but shock after shock succeeded till my whole frame seemed literally consumed with fire; and yet it was not like the fire that we use daily, [for] if we touch it will immediately give great pain. This was heavenly fire, and filled me with joy unspeakable." For him and all the others previously cited, these were moments like unto that time when the finger of the Lord touched those sixteen stones for the Brother of Jared, causing them to glow continuously day and night in light or dark. What they all felt was the same divine substance or element that went into each of those small molten glass rocks, namely, some of the heavenly virtue should always be attached to the holy priesthood of the Son of God.

This holy element of the priesthood is illuminating, radiating, glowing, brilliantly transparent, and very much like a subdued fire with its wonderfully electric sensation that thrills through a body's central nervous system, muscle tissue and utmost extremities, totally sanctifying whatever it comes into contact with. This is precisely what the Lord Jesus Christ imparted from His own spiritual tabernacle, which was then clothed with an outer hologram pattern of what His mortal body would eventually resemble, to those wonderful stones on Mount Shalem/Mount T'ai Shan in eastern China. No wonder then that Apostle Orson Pratt, upon blessing some virgin olive oil one time to be used in the administration of the sick, prayed thusly over it: "And may thy finger O Lord, touch this oil now and impart unto it the same type of virtue which thou didst put into each one of those stones for the Brother of Jared; that this oil may give life, even as they gave light..." (as recorded in the Diary of Charlotte Bradley of Moroni, UT, under the date of July 19th, 1970, which statement she attributed to Church Patriarch John Smith, whom she once served as a scribe to in her youth; this information was given in a Moroni ward High Priests' Quorum by her at the invitation of Merlin Nielsen; this author found her diary among many other personal effects at the Moroni City garbage dump shortly after her demise and has kept it in his possession ever since).

Of those sixteen stones that the Brother of Jared and his people brought with them across the water to North America, only one seems to have survived over the last four millenniums, the other fifteen being unaccounted for at this time. The history surrounding its rediscovery is just as incredible as the stone itself. An early Latter-day Saint by the name of Edwin Rushton was at home resting one afternoon in early May, 1846 when he had an "open vision" in broad daylight. He was led "to a ravine a few blocks south of the Nauvoo Temple" by the Holy Spirit and shown within a depth of five feet below the surface "a pot of treasure on top of which was a record of plates about three by six inches in measurement. On top of these plates was a beautiful seer stone, clear as crystal..." With the kind assistance of three other priesthood brethren, he obtained that stone on May 4th by digging at the same spot he had seen in vision; he left the treasure and plates, however, being unable to retrieve them for some strange reason. The hole was refilled and he kept the stone in his possession. He used it from time to time to help other church members locate lost articles or other things of great value to them. "The stone is described as being about the size of a hen's egg, having the appearance of molten glass, light sea green in color, irregular of surface, nearly kidney-shaped with wrinkles or hieroglyphic marks, called 'the rising sun,' on a concave surface."

Apostle James E. Talmage, a geologist by training, was once invited to inspect Edwin Rushton's seerstone by his wife when he called at her home in company with Angus M. Cannon on February 21st, 1893. "To my surprise Sister Rushton suggested that we take the stone with us, and have it tested. Pres. Cannon advised me to take it. While examining it in the house of Bro. Rushton, a tiny flake, scarcely larger than a grain of wheat, fell off from an end. This I took care of, intending to use it for a simple chemical test. During the afternoon I made a careful examination of the stone. It is transparent, of a greenish tinge, low fusibility and hardness, specific quantity of 2.5, contains silica. And the alkalies, in fact, appear to the eye and under test to be a piece of glass, plain and simple. It weighs 66 grams (nearly two and one fourth oz.). The chemical tests were confined to the flake which broke off in our hands, as I did not wish to mutilate the stone in any way. This determination of the simple lithological nature of these stones in no way to my mind removes the possibility of them possessing unusual virtues."

The stone is quite ancient and has its origins with the Brother of Jared on Mount Shalem, where it along with 15 others, were touched by the finger of the Lord himself. This egg-size stone of "molten glass" has been used a number of times since its discovery by certain faithful men and women possessed of seership capabilities to find lost objects, people, or animals, usually with very good success. It is presently in private hands, but could very easily work again for anyone worthy enough to operate it by childlike faith, submissive humility, and unlimited compassion. For this seerstone still contains the inert virtue that once illuminated it with life and light for the benefit of traveling Jaredites. And that virtue can be unlocked at any given time under the right kind of circumstances.

Consider what happened in ancient times with the Old Testament prophet Elisha. He was a man obviously filled with a great deal of this eternal priesthood element in life, as evidenced by the many great miracles he performed for others. Upon his death, as written in II Kings 13:20-21, his body was entombed in the usual

160

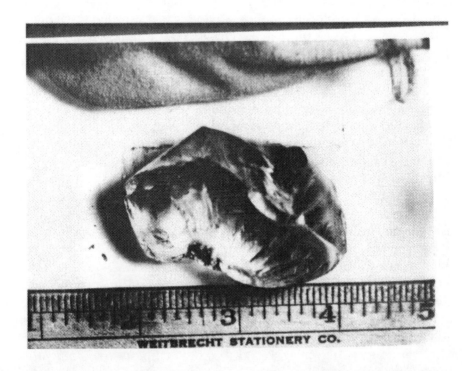

One of the sixteen "molten" glass stones made by the Brother of Jared in ancient times and taken up to the top of a sacred mountain where the finger of the Lord touched each of them, thereby imparting some of His own priesthood virtue for them to become luminescent. It was rediscovered through vision and excavated near the Nauvoo temple by Edwin Rushton on May 4th, 1846. It is currently in private hands in southern Utah somewhere.

sepulcher reserved for such purposes. In time, the elements of nature claimed the flesh of his corpse, leaving only the skeletal remains behind. Now a band of marauding Moabites had invaded the land "at the coming in of [a certain] year." One of their number was slain and in making a hasty retreat "they cast the [dead] man into the sepulcher of Elisha; and when the man was let down, and touched the bones of Elisha, he revived and stood on his feet" on account of the priesthood virtue which still remained in the prophet's weathered bones. One who has handled the Rushston's seerstone in the past, with faith and priesthood virtue in himself, declared to me in all soberness that "an electric sensation thrilled through my system, and I was astonished to see the stone give off a flickering soft light for a few moments." But the good brother's surprise turned to fear and the moment that happened, the stone's brief luminescence quickly evaporated. (The foregoing information concerning the Jaredite glow-stone found by Edwin Rushton in Nauvoo comes from the following several sources: Kate B. Carter, *Our Pioneer Heritage* (SLC: Daughters of Utah Pioneers, 1964; 7:575-576; *James E. Talmage Journals* 6:87-90, Lee Library, Special Collections, box 27, folder 4, BYU; the *Journal of Edwin Rushton*, p. 3; William Evans Perkes' *History of Richard Rushton, Sr. & Family* (Alhambra, CA: Greenwood Press, 1977; p. 31); Ogden Kraut's *Seers and Seerstones* (Dugway, UT: n.d. [no date]; pp. 45-61); *Journal of Mary Ellen Kimball* (SLC: Pioneer Press, 1994; pp. 65-66); *Frederick Kesler Diary*, entry for March 12th, 1882, Western Americana, Univ. of Utah, SLC; and an oral interview with Patriarch William E. Perkes of Fillmore, Utah on Friday, October 25th, 1985.)

CHAPTER TWELVE

ASCENDING THE MOUNTAIN OF HOLINESS: LOCATING THE PARTICULAR PEAK IN FARAWAY CHINA WHERE THE BROTHER OF JARED MET THE LORD JESUS CHRIST

In the latter part of the turbulent 1970's when our family still resided in Manti, Utah, and my friendship with John Brewer was at its peak, I read something one day in what was then the official organ of the Church, the *Improvement Era* (30(4):314; February, 1927). The items had been submitted by an old Manti resident, one L. A. Wilson and is reproduced here in its entirety:

"Students of the Book of Mormon are always on the lookout for any item in history or science bearing upon that record, and so the following is submitted: An account of the tradition among the Chinese, of their first settlement in China, seems to hint at that remarkable migration of the Jaredites from the Tower of Babel to the 'great sea which divides the lands,' where some of them (doubtless only a part of them) took to the barges which were lighted in so remarkable a manner. Dr. Fisher, of Yale, gives this account:–

"'The nucleus of the Chinese nation is thought to have been a band of immigrants, who are supposed by some to have crossed the headwaters of the Oxus. They followed the course of the Hoang Ho, or Yellow River, having entered the country of their adoption from the northwest, and they planted themselves in the present province of Shan-se.'

"Further to identify these people to the Book of Mormon reader, Dr. Fisher adds, 'Although nomads, they had some knowledge of astronomy.' Of the occurrences while the migration halted at that point, history, of course, says nothing. But the annual pilgrimage of hundreds of thousands of Chinese to the top of their sacred mountain just at the point of the peninsula of Shantung testifies to the Book of

Mormon student very eloquently of the wonderful manifestations received there by the brother of Jared."

Not long after reading this, an opportunity was presented to me by a medical colleague to join him and some others on a scientific tour to the People's Republic of China. This was shortly after President Richard Nixon's famous "ping-pong diplomacy" which sent an American team over there to match their skills with a group of equally good Chinese ping-pong players. The group we would be going with, he indicated in a letter to me, would actually be only the second group of Americans permitted back into Red China since the Communists gained control of that country back in the late 1940s and drove the Nationalists over to the tiny island of Formosa (now Taiwan) where they finally took refuge. The organization sponsoring this tour was the American Medical Students' Association in concert with the Ministry of Health in Beijing. My invited participation with four medical doctors and 29 third- and fourth-year medical students was because of my extensive knowledge of Chinese culture, history and, more particularly, its traditional medicine.

It was a 21-day excursion that straddled the two mid-summer months of July and August in 1980. We first had to go through another Communist country before flying directly into Red China, so we made a little necessary side into Ethiopia for a couple days. The China experience was for me a double blessing—the advantage of visiting clinics and hospitals where herbal medicine and acupuncture were regularly used alongside surgery and prescription drugs, and visiting the place spoken of in the *Improvement Era* article.

Our prearranged travel itinerary was pretty much set in stone, or, at least, so I was told. But where there is a deserving will, there is invariably a foreordained way to make it happen. In this case, my way to Mount T'ai Shan—one of five of China's most sacred mountains in the Shandong Province situated halfway between Beijing and Shanghai—was through a couple of the Manti metal plates which Brewer permitted me to take with and two inscrutable officials at the Ministry of Culture, Office of Artifacts somewhere in Beijing's Forbidden City.

Referring to my journal under the entries for late July and early August of 1980, I discovered that one of our group's government-appointed interpreters by the name of Xiao-Ping helped in the facilitation of my much-desired side trip to T'ai Shan. I showed them two of the lead plates from the old cave somewhat northeast of Manti. Two older, bespectacled gentlemen with whom we conferred, turned out to be the Directors of this Office of Artifacts. They examined both lead plates very carefully beneath a magnifying glass with some thoughtful reverence and a few whispered awes of surprise. Finally, one of them went over to a battered filing cabinet in one corner of their sparsely-furnitured office, lifted a manila folder out of the top drawer and returned to the desk that we all sat around.

I was shown some color and black-and-white photos of a number of different Chinese oracle bones on which were inscribed numerous Neolithic characters. As I compared these incised markings with those on the two Manti plates, I could quickly see the reason for the contained excitement from both officials. The inscriptions on both artifacts bore an uncanny resemblance to each other. It's almost as if the same scribe had written both sets of characters. Here, for me, was living archaeological proof that at some time in the very ancient past, the Chinese and the Jaredites were one and the same race.

I didn't need an explanation through my interpreter from either of these bureaucrats relative to the oracle bones, since I already knew something about their ancient history. Between 1928 and 1937, China's principal scholarly organization, the Academia Sinica, excavated 15 separate sites in the Anyang area of Honan Province, some 310 miles south of Beijing. During this 10-year campaign, the excavators uncovered a total of nearly 20,000 oracle bones. This huge collection proved to be the most significant single source of material for the oracle-bone studies that would follow in the ensuing decades.

The oracle bone inscriptions represent the earliest-known evidence of Chinese writing that belonged to China's first great cultural period, then ruled by the Shang Dynasty. Their realm in the second millennium B.C. extended from what is now Liaoning Province in northern China westward to what is now Shensi Province and thence southward below the Yangtze River. Other oracle-bone discoveries made in the late 1970s imply that Shang authority even extended 744 miles further south of the capital, Anyang in Honan Province. Back 4,000 years ago, Shang aristocrats enjoyed seeking the frequent advice from some of their dearly-departed ancestors. This form of supernatural inquiry was managed through divination.

The divining technique called for the preparation of "oracle bones," most commonly the shoulder blade of an ox or the plastron (bottom shell) of a turtle. However, the process wasn't just limited to these items, but also included the shoulder blades of goats and sheep, pieces of antler, and even human cranial bones sometimes. After an oracle bone had been prepared, the diviner engraved his questions on its smoothed surface, exposed the bone (or the shell) to heat and then judged from the cracks that appeared afterwards whether the oracular answers to his questions were favorable or otherwise. The easiest and most preferred method of preparation was to soak steer bones or turtle shells in either wine or vinegar, which made them much easier to engrave inscriptions upon. These oracle bones suggest that not only did the Shang Dynasty initiate the first writing system, but also introduced the yin-yang or balance concept as well as ancestral worship into Chinese philosophy.

Through my interpreter Xiao-Ping, I told both gentlemen that my chief purpose in wanting to go down and visit Mount T'ai Shan was to investigate a published hypothesis (the Era article) about the first great Chinese leader (Mahonri Moriancumer) making communication with the gods (in this case the Lord Jesus Christ) up there and returning with illuminated stones that glowed in the dark. Upon hearing this, both men became visibly excited and told us that they were somewhat acquainted with the old legends regarding this, and would readily give their permission to make my side trip possible. The Travel Service Bureau was promptly notified of a sudden change in plans for at least one member of our group, to which they grudgingly but quickly complied.

Quoting from a portion of my lengthy journal entry under the date of Thursday, July 24th, 1980, I expressed my deep-felt joy at the final outcome of our visit to this bureau. "Naturally, when the good news reached my ears, I felt extremely grateful in my heart to Almighty God for what I consider to be A MIGHTY MIRACLE wrought in my behalf. Not so much an exuberance as a deep calm sense of modest joy and peaceful pleasure in my God and the tremendous faith which He endowed me with at an early age." All of the seemingly insurmountable obstacles that had stood in my way before to bar me from separating from the rest of my medical group to make this necessary journey, had finally melted away like so many big blocks of cold, uninviting ice.

166

One of the lead plates from the old Jaredite cave in Manti, Ut. Compare the inscriptions on it with those on a 4,000-year-old oracle bone from eastern China.

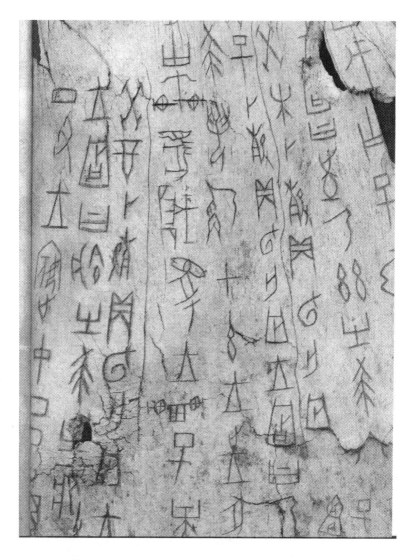

An oracle-bone inscription made on the shoulder blade of a sheep. This ancient relic was unearthed in the vicinity of Anyang, the last Shang capital, in Honan province, about 310 miles south of Beijing. Note that these characters bear a strong resemblance to the inscriptions found on the lead plate from the old Jaredite cave in Manti, Utah.

What the reader must bear in mind here is that at that time mainland China was still pretty much closed to most foreigners and was just beginning to open a crack with selected groups like the American ping-pong players and our medical students and accompanying faculty. Presently, just about anyone can visit that country and go almost anywhere his or her heart desires, devoid of the tight restrictions and tough policies that faced us two decades ago.

I shall skip over other obstacles which Satan seemed to be throwing across my path after this, such as coming down with a sudden case of ptomaine food poisoning at a duck dinner held in our honor. Or the drenching downpour from an unexpected cloudburst that appeared out of nowhere while climbing Mount T'ai Shan, that thoroughly soaked my guide Chou Yu-Tsun and I to the bone. Nor will I even bother mentioning the surprising inflammation that set into my right kneecap the next morning, crippling me up with such excruciating pain that I had to swallow my pride and consent to the embarrassment of being carried down from that mountain top on a stretcher by two young men.

The point is that I made the ascent in one piece, though a little rougher for the physical wear and tear that my poor body encountered along the way. Rather than quoting again from some more lengthy journal entries, I will selectively summarize some of the more important things which happened to me up there late Sunday night of July 27th. Before doing so I wish to give the reader a little historical background on what makes this particular mountain peak so holy and special to the older Chinese generation. I derive my information from Edwin Bernbaum's classic work, *Sacred Mountains of The World* (San Francisco: Sierra Club Books, 1990; pp. 30-35). "As the eastern peak, it receives the first light of the sun, the divine source of all life. The mysterious power that refreshes and revitalizes the body and spirit of all living things flows through the sacred peak, shining forth from its summit in the first magic glow of dawn. For thousands of years Chinese writers have eulogized T'ai Shan as the supreme mountain, surpassing all others in spiritual height and significance.

"The emperors of China regarded T'ai Shan as the son of the Emperor of Heaven, from whom they received their mandate to rule. He functioned for them as an important deity deputized to attend to the affairs of this world and to communicate their wishes to the supreme ruler on high. As the earthly representative of the Emperor of Heaven, T'ai Shan became the greatest of all the terrestrial gods, over whom he ruled through an immense bureaucracy. He assumed the role of divine arbiter of life and death. The Chinese believed that the souls of those who died went to a hill at the foot of the peak. There T'ai Shan himself passed judgment on the good and evil a person had done in his or her life. The expression 'going to T'ai Shan' became a common euphemism for dying. As the peak of the east endowed with the power of dawn, the mountain was also regarded as the source or the shaper of life. Through underlings occupying a maze of offices that made up his massive bureaucracy, T'ai Shan determined everything that would happen to a person—birth, position, honor, fortune, and death. Until the Communist Revolution in 1949, every village of any importance had a temple dedicated to the divine ruler of the sacred mountain—and one of the largest and most important temples in Beijing, the Temple of the Eastern Peak, was devoted to his worship. Because of its great importance in the life of the Chinese people, T'ai Shan has a longer record of ascents than any other mountain on earth."

After my guide and I had finally managed to reach the top amid considerable struggles and hardships on account of the slippery conditions and a thorough soaking for both of us due to a tremendous cloudburst, we found the view from the mountain's sacred heights to be wonderfully inspiring and, in language that's fairly typical of most Mormon missionaries, "totally awesome." Viewing everything through this portal of Heaven, reduced the human world and all of its puny accomplishments below to an absolute nothing, or mathematically speaking to a dull zero!

We got ourselves situated in a hotel built by the government on the highest peak, where our clothing and gear got dried out. From my journal diligently kept on this historic journey, I extract the following: "We slept for a few hours. Boy! was that bed ever a welcome sight when I dropped into it for awhile. To my weary, aching body and sore bones, it was heaven on earth, and probably as near true heaven as one could ever hope to get in the physical sense of the word."

After a late supper, I donned a heavy quilted jacket and informed my guide, Sun, that I was off to explore some of the other peaks a short distance away. I selected the plainest and what seemed the least-visited peak, where I found a simple pavilion made of hewn

The ancient pilgrimage route to the South Gate of heaven that sits atop Mount T'ai Shan. Legends about its extreme sacredness undoubtedly spring from the Brother of Jared's historic ascent to the top in ancient times where he conversed with the Lord Jesus Christ (see Ether 3 in the *Book of Mormon*). Legend has it that the very first Chinese emperor went to the top and prayed to the gods, who illuminated some glass stones for him. When he came down, he placed them in different temples of worship.

stone covered over by a simple pagoda-style roof supported by four columns. I waited until darkness came and everyone else had vacated the area before I settled myself down into a meditative state of peace and composure. In my journal I noted this: "I watched as clouds gathered around the top of the mount itself, until eventually no lights from the hotel or village on the next peak over, or from the city of Tian below, could be seen. I was literally enveloped in a heavy mist of clouds, which stayed there for the total duration of my prayers unto God. At which time they ended (I surmised about 1 a.m. Monday morning), the clouds all blew away and the lights of man's dwellings again became present before me.

"I was prompted by the Spirit of God in me at the time, to first of all sanctify the entire simple edifice under which I then was, as well as the immediate surrounding vicinity, which I did by virtue of the holy priesthood that I hold. After having done this, I commenced one of the most lengthy and soul-satisfying prayers I have ever uttered in my entire life. It must have lasted several hours for my body ached in various places from so much kneeling and bending over. Periodically, I would have to pause long enough to get up and stretch a little and walk around some to help ease muscle cramps and joint stiffness before resuming my former position of humble worship."

The thought occurred to me at that time that Mount T'ai Shan was indeed the very Mount Shalem (Ether 3:1) to which the Brother of Jared ascended and communicated with the Lord. Formed a long, long time ago from a weathered intrusion of granite magma, it sits solidly on the earth with a sense of immovable power and majesty, like a king or emperor seated on his gilded throne. Ridges embroidered with intricate patterns of pines and cedars spread out from its flanks like the folds of one of our Mormon temple robes. Steep slopes of gray rock, cut here and there by precipitous cliffs, emerge from its lower ramparts to stand out against the sky.

"So this is where Mahonri Moriancumer came to speak with our Savior," I thoughtfully mused, while taking another short walk between my long prayer. The faith of this great man must have been truly incredible! "Nowhere in the scriptures do we have an example of more perfect faith," wrote Kent P. Jackson, a professor of ancient scriptures at BYU, in *Volume 8 of Studies in Scripture: Alma 30 to Moroni* (Salt Lake City: Deseret Book Co., 1988; p. 254). His trip to such a lofty sanctified place as this was no different than Enoch's own ascent to Mount Simeon (Moses 7:2), located somewhere on the other side to the west of the Garden of Eden in Jackson County, Missouri (according to Joseph Smith), Noah's preach-and-gratitude offering on top of Ararat, or Moses' separate ascents to Mounts Horeb and Sinai on different occasions to learn the mind and will of God concerning his future as well as that of those whom he led. Here were mighty men of granite-hardened faith meeting their Redeemer under various situations and for different reasons. Yet each of them prevailed with the Lord in such a way that nothing could be kept from their view. They were, even as Father Abraham was, sons of might and faith, belonging to an ancient order of priesthood older than the earth itself. For them God was something real and tangible and not as with most of us today, a "warm and cuddly" figment of our own perverse imaginations. It was the equivalent of a solid handshake when deal is struck between two individuals—the one comes with childlike faith and humility and the other manifests with power and glory in ways no human tongue can tell or hand describe in written words. It was, still is, and will always be the ultimate consummation between imperfect mortality and perfected divinity. The union, the love, the peace, and power which such oneness generates is overwhelming but very, very soul-satisfying. It is the 'electric chair' of spirituality that melts away darkness and sin without 'frying' the brain and central nervous system or stopping the heart. Such an experience is, indeed, both electrifying and illuminating all at once. It is like 'radiant fire' shut up within a person's tabernacle that conveys a sense of physical lightness devoid of the heavy draw that gravity exerts.

All of this and much, much more is what the Brother of Jared felt while in a fully prostrated position upon the ground. And in a considerably far less sense, it, too, was something I experienced, only in a more subtle way. Former Church President Lorenzo Snow was blessed by Patriarch Isaac Morley in Nauvoo with "the great faith of the Brother of Jared" and the promise that some of his "sons shall be large and mighty men, even large in stature like the Jaredites" and possessing "the strength of Samson" (see Isaac Morley's *Patriarchal Blessing Book*, Book E, p. 71).

CHAPTER THIRTEEN

A RACE OF GIANTS IN THE LAND

Besides the obvious place of China to look for evidence of the ancient Jaredites, there are also lesser known regions within the Americas, particularly in the western part of North America and our own home state. On the morning of August 25th, 1865, according to *The Deseret News* (14(48):1; August 30, 1865), "Presidents B. Young and Heber C. Kimball of the First Presidency, and Elders Wilford Woodruff, Geo. A. Smith, Franklin D. Richards and Geo. Q. Cannon of the Twelve Apostles, with other brethren and sisters, left G. S. L. City at 9 o'clock, to hold a two-day meeting in Tooele City..." where they received a grand and cordial welcome.

In the Saturday afternoon session, wrote Elder Woodruff in his journal, "Joseph F. Smith spoke well [and] the Spirit & mantle of the prophets was upon him" (see *Wilford Woodruff's Journal* 6:241 under August 26th, 1865 entry). The News commented that Elder Smith "discoursed upon what constitutes a true minister of the gospel, and showed that example coupled with precept is required by the Lord and by His people of every man who is a true minister of Christ."

The Sunday morning session began at 10 a.m. Heber C. Kimball noted that "it is our duty to be honest, upright and true in all of our feelings with one another and with all men" everywhere. Then Apostle George A. Smith weighed in (all 300 pounds of him) with some preliminary remarks about the Jaredites. "The men that came out from the great Tower were powerful men and occupied the land for thirty generations. They had among them prophets to teach them the way of the Lord. But they finally forsook the Lord and drew the sword against each other. The Lord sent prophets unto them, but they would not hearken to their words. Coriantumr, who was King over all the land in the days of Ether the Prophet, contended with the factions that opposed him. But he relented in his feelings at the shedding of blood, and offered his kingdom to Shiz. [But Shiz] would not consent to stop

175

the shedding of blood unless Coriantumr would suffer himself to be slain by Shiz. This was not consented to, and though two million men had been slain, the wars again commenced and continued until all were slain, except Coriantumr, and the prophet Ether, who recorded it. This was the fulfillment of a prophecy of Ether." Elder Smith was of the opinion that their remains could be found in many locations, including right there in Tooele.

Shortly before the arrival of this entourage of important church leaders, two young teenage boys, Orson W. Huntsman and David O. Huntsman, were out roaming around on a 10-mile stretch of grassy bench land situated between their father's big ranch and the town of Tooele. Now bordering this wide grassy region were surrounding hills that carried evident marks of the ancient shoreline of old Lake Bonneville. They were eager to explore around on this terrace to satisfy their own innate curiosities.

As they looked upward to a hill just above them, they noticed from a certain angle a hole in the side of it. With renewed excitement, they eagerly scrambled up to the entrance and discovered about ten feet inside, something very old, dry, and shriveled up. It looked to them like an old discarded "squash," which is what they called it. They continued further in and found themselves inside a very high and wide cavern of ancient origins. Excited beyond words, they took their "squash" with them and returned home to show their parents the mysterious find.

When Brigham Young and the other apostles arrived in Tooele a short time later, this "squash" was taken to him for further evaluation, accompanied with a written explanation of how it was found. President Young turned the curious object over in his hands a number of times as he examined it from all sides, while meditatively pondering on the matter at the same time. Finally, he broke his silence with a short statement to the effect that this supposed "old squash" was, in reality, the skull of an ancient Jaredite.

He and some of the others expressed a desire to meet the boys who made this discovery and accompany them to the place where it was first located. Given the propensity of cockiness in youth, the two Huntsman boys and their egos retched up several notches higher as they led the Prophet of the Lord and other servants of God back to the well-hidden cavern. With the air being in short supply and virtually no circulation inside the rock chamber, great care had to be taken going in. Torches were lit at the entrance way, and several men held aloft a wagon cover to create just enough air movement underneath, so they could continue burning while providing ample breathing space for those going inside.

The men had to move very slowly so as not to stir up several inches of yellow human dust that covered much of the cavern floor. The walls were lined with a number of stone shelves containing numerous skeletal remains. Awe and wonderment undoubtedly filled the minds of those privileged to see such ancient evidence for themselves. Finally, Prophet Young broke the spell-binding silence by declaring that "there were bones of the Jaredites, well a long time" (see Lamond W. Huntsman's *Huntsman Annals* (Provo: J. Grant Stevenson, 1971; pp. 46-47). It has been estimated that between 10 and 15 million Jaredites were eventually slaughtered in the final great battles fought around the vicinity of the Hill Cumorah in upstate New York (see *Edward Stevenson Journal* 36:2 under the entry for December 17th, 1888). Perhaps those large numbers of skeletons found near Tooele by Young and company could have been unfortunate victims of some of these eastward migrating conflicts.

An even more remarkable find of Jaredite skeletal remains occurred many years ago in Utah County. It was sometime in the mid-1930s when Utah Lake dropped to its lowest water levels ever, due to several years of virtually no moisture to speak of. A self-trained naturalist-geologist-archaeologist from nearby Lehi by the name of John Hutchings (then in his mid-forties), was able to walk out a good distance on dry lake bed where he located and excavated several large mounds. While digging into one of them near the lake's epicenter (that would normally have been under many feet of water), he struck what he assumed to be a large rock. But in the process of further digging around, his slight annoyance turned to amazement as he discovered a portion of an ancient, rounded, cemented stone roof that had once been covered with a pitch-like substance (apparently for waterproofing).

He had a small rock hammer and a pointed trowel with him in addition to his shovel. Patiently he worked away enough stone with these implements to form a hole large enough through which he could enter. Hutchings never went on any exploratory trip without taking along some matches and a miner's coal-oil lantern as well as adequate water and a little dried fruit to drink or much on whenever he became hungry or thirsty. He now realized just how handy that lantern would come in. But before lighting it, he walked several feet directly across from his first hole, dug another one and pried away some more stone. This now gave him both an entry and exit through which air could travel to keep his lantern from going out.

Once it was lit, he lowered it through the first opening and leaned in to have a better look. He gauged the distance to the floor to be only four feet, having been lucky enough to penetrate through on the room's circular perimeters instead of going in further towards the top, where the descent would have been much greater and probably required a rope (which he didn't have with him at the time) to do so. Once safely inside, he moved towards the center of the chamber where there was more head room and he could straighten up from his stooped position. A large stone box sealed with a heavy lid about the size of a small coffin sat in front of him. As he gradually turned around, the light reflecting off the walls revealed 12 very large skeletons carefully laid out around the stone chest in a clockwise arrangement, with the skulls facing inward towards the box.

Taking a tape measure from his trouser pocked, he measured several of the skeletons from head to foot with the lantern on the floor beside him. He was astonished by the measurements taken: eight-feet-four-inches for one; eight-feet-eleven-inches for another; and nine-feet-four-inches for a third. When my father took my brother and I, as young teenagers, out to visit Mr. Hutchings on July 21st, 1961, during the time of this spell-binding narrative, the 72-year-old gentleman paused long enough to remind us that it helps, at times like this, if one is a little clairvoyant. He told us that he was and had inherited this gift from his own father as a young child. Mr. Hutchings said that while he was inside what seemed to be an old burial chamber, his mind was trying to figure out what civilization had produced such giants as these. Just then a flash of intelligence crossed his mind with the idea that these were all Jaredite skeletons.

He next examined the stone chest itself and found by measuring its various dimensions to be thirty inches long, sixteen inches wide, and eighteen inches tall. As he thoughtfully paused to give some consideration to removing the sealed lid for an inspection of the

An ancient stone box from the Jaredite mummy cave near Manti, Utah. Originally these boxes were wrapped in juniper bark and sealed over with pitch pine to make them water tight.

The same small stone box with more of the bark and resin covering removed.

(Photos courtesy of Terry Carter)

179

This is the same stone box with all of its exterior fiber-and-resin covering removed. These are some of the metal plates with inscriptions found inside.

An overhead view of the same stone box minus its metal records. The construction of such a box closely resembles the much larger one which John Hutchings found in a very old burial mound located in the middle of Utah Lake after the water had receded.

(Photos courtesy of Terry Carter)

Metal plates found inside the ancient stone box from the Jaredite cave in Sanpete County, Utah. When the rectangular lid was still intact, it was held in place by a small wooden dowel which ran down through one wall of the box with a protruding end fitting snugly into a small notch made in the rim of the lid. The lid would easily swing open to the left or right when moved by hand. The metal plates that were found inside and shown here are very similar to those which John Hutchings suspected were in the stone box he found inside that circule of huge skeletons sometime in the mid-1930's.

(Photo courtesy of Terry Carter)

contents inside, a feeling ebbed over him that such an act would be wrong to do. But a general disclosure of what the chest did contain was brought to his mind. He was given to understand that it contained a number of different metallic records giving the life histories of each of these individuals, all of whom apparently belonged to a royal family of some kind. This had been their burial chamber where the deceased members were interred. As he pondered the propriety of removing some of the remains themselves, a good feeling descended over him as an indication that such a thing was permissible.

He left the tomb and walked some distance back to his truck and retrieved half-a-dozen shaved wood bushel baskets with lids that fit over their wire handles. Orchard growers used these to shore their picked apples, peaches, and pears in, but Mr. Hutchings used them to carry things that he found on his various jaunts, such as bird nests, Indian arrowheads and spear points, pottery shards, willow baskets, grass sandals, and rock and mineral specimens. He returned to the tomb and carefully placed six of the complete skeletons into each bushel basket. He remarked to my father, brother and I in his narration that the arm bones were so long on some of these skeletons, "the hand-and-finger bones almost reached the kneecaps on a few of them." He closed up both holes after exiting the chamber and made sure all evidence of human presence in the area was obliterated before leaving the spot. He gave three skeletons to the University of Utah and two others to Brigham Young University, keeping the best one of the bunch for himself. He told professors at both schools how he came by way of them, but instead of winning their compliments, he suffered their scorn and ridicule. "They just laughed at me, saying there was no such thing in the middle of Utah Lake," my father later recorded in his unpublished life's history. "After that I wanted nothing more to do with professors or educated men" (taken from "My Life's Journal" by Jacob Heinerman, pp. 31-37).

An early LDS newspaper, *The Evening and Morning Star* (1(3):22; August 1832) identified exceptionally large skeletons (like those previously referred to in this text) as being ancient Jaredites: "...As they were a very large race of men, whenever we hear that uncommon large bones have been dug up from the earth, we may conclude, that was the skeleton of a Jaredite! Outside of the Beehive State, skeletons of gigantic proportions have been found in other parts of America, including some along the Western Reserve (a tract of land in NE Ohio, on the southern shore of Lake Erie).

From the *Journal History of the Church* under September 8th, 1880 (p. 3) is a clipping from the *Cincinnati (Ohio) Enquirer* about an excavated mound in Muskingum County filled with giant remains. "In one grave, there were two skeletons – one male and one female. The male skeleton measured nine feet in length, and the female eight feet. In another grave were also found two skeletons – male and female. The male frame in this case was nine feet four inches in length, and the female eight feet. In another grave was found a female skeleton, holding in her arms the skeleton of a child three feet and a half long. [A] remaining seven [skeletons] were found in single graves, and were lying on their sides. The smallest of the seven was nine feet in length, and the largest ten."

Solomon Spaulding, the one time clergyman-turned-disbeliever, who wrote the famous *Spaulding Manuscript*, received at least a part of his creative inspiration from some huge Jaredite remains found on his land one time. (Some of Joseph Smith's bitterest foes accused him of copying the Book of Mormon directly from Spaulding's own manuscript, since there are a few slight similarities between the two of them. Nothing could be further from the truth, however.) The reverend's daughter, M.S. McKinstry granted an exclusive interview to *Scribner's Monthly* (20(4):615; August 1880) on the matter of her father's work.

"During the war of 1812, I was residing with my parents in a little town in Ohio called Conneaut. I was then in my sixth year. My father was in business there, and I remember his iron foundry and the men he had at work. But he remained at home most of the time, and was reading and writing a great deal. He frequently wrote little stories which he read to me. There were some round mounds of earth near our house which greatly interested him. He said a tree on top of one of them was a thousand years old. He set some of his men to work digging into one of these mounds. I vividly remember how excited he became when he heard that they had exhumed some human bones, portions of gigantic skeletons, and various relics. He talked with my mother of these discoveries in the mound, and was writing every day as the work progressed."

Today, physical evidence for the existence of ancient Jaredites may still be found, but you just have to look a little harder for it in some of the less obvious places. Take, for instance, the cattle that are so common to ranches throughout the Americas. (This would include those 30,000 cattle that the LDS Church runs on its own private 300,000-acre Florida ranch near Melbourne that's now conservatively valued at $858 million, and generates an annual pre-tax revenue in the neighborhood of $10 million. See the restricted, confidential *History of Deseret Ranches of Florida 1950-1989* (p. 30) by D. Delos Ellsworth; and Richard N. and Joah K. Ostlings' *Mormon America: The Power and The Promise* (San Francisco: HarperCollins Publishers, 1999; p. 121.) Well, the native cattle that started these vast herds many decades ago originally came across the ocean in those eight Jaredite barges mentioned in the Book of Ether. At least, so said Jared Carter, an early Mormon elder of some note, in his private journal: "There is no account given in the Book of Mormon that the people of Lehi brought any cattle with them or any beast of any kind. But the Book of Mormon tells us that the Jaredites brought cattle over onto this land. And when the Jaredites were destroyed, many of their cattle were left in the south countries. And when the people of Lehi came over, they brought no cattle with them. But when and where they landed, they found all sorts of cattle" (see *Jared Carter Journals*, pp. 174-176).

Now these Jaredite bulls and cows came with their masters from the Great Tower on the vast plains of Shinar. They were domesticated stock which originated from herds of large-sized, wild cattle that roamed free in those times (see *Natural History* 71(6):37 (June-July 1962). But once they brought to this Western Hemisphere, there began a gradual but "progressive diminution of size," as the larger species slowly became extinct and was eventually replaced with smaller phyletic substitutes, comparable in size to our own present cattle breeds (see Karl W. Butzer's *Environment and Archaeology: An Ecological Approach to Prehistory* (2nd Ed.), p. 505).

Some of the antiquarian city, county, and state histories of the early 19th century contain occasional references to extraordinary-sized human remains. Case in point would be Harvey Rice's *Pioneers of the Western Reserve* (p. 303), in which he described an ancient burial ground that was uncovered in 1800. Concerning the giant skeletons found in this particular Ohio mound, we read: "Human bones of gigantic proportions were discovered in such a state of preservation as to be accurately described and measured. The cavities of the skulls were large enough in their dimensions to receive the entire head of a man of modern times, and could be put on one's head with as much ease as a hat or cap. The jaw-bones were sufficiently large to admit being placed so as to match or fit the outside of a modern man's face. The other bones, so far as discovered, appeared to be of equal proportions with the skulls and jaw-bones. Several of [these] have been preserved as relics in the cabinets of antiquarians, where they may still be seen."

But what good are such huge skeletons without "some flesh on them bones?" There once was in the last century just past, a living specimen of what a real Jaredite may have been like (though the man himself wasn't genetically related at all to the others). His name was Robert Wadlow and he was born of normal parents. "At age 8, Robert was already six feet tall; by the time he was 13 he was over seven feet tall. When he died in 1940, at the age of 30, Robert Wadlow wore a size 25 ring, had an arm span of nine feet, weighed 440 pounds, wore a size 37AA shoe, and was eight feet eleven inches tall. Willie Camper, another giant from Memphis, TN, measured eight feet five inches tall. His hand was over twelve inches long, from his wrist to the tip of his middle finger. He could hold a dozen eggs unstacked in the palm of his hand." (Copied from an exhibit display at Ripley's 'Believe It or Not' Museum in Orlando, FL during a visit there on Friday, January 3, 1997.)

The Jaredites were THE greatest civilization the world has ever known. They ruled for nearly 19 centuries as the sole, undisputed occupants of the ENTIRE Western Hemisphere. In his small tract, "Remarkable Visions" (Liverpool: R. James, Printer, July 14th, 1849; no. 5, p. 7), Apostle Orson Pratt effectively summarized their accomplishments (as well as ultimate downfall) this way: "[God] promised to make them a great and powerful nation, so that there should be no greater nation upon all the face of the earth. Accordingly, in process of time, they became a numerous and powerful people, occupying principally North America; building large cities in all quarters of the land; being a civilized and enlightened nation. Agriculture and machinery were carried on to a great extent. Commercial and manufacturing business flourished on every hand; yet, in consequence of wickedness they were entirely destroyed; leaving their houses, their cities, and their land desolate, and their sacred records [buried]."

The best witness to the world's greatest nation may be found in that section of The Book of Mormon known as the Book of Ether. In some 32 pages of written history is recorded the might and failures of these incredible giants. Listen to the words which the last Jaredite prophet, Ether, wrote concerning his people, and which the last Nephite prophet, Moroni abbreviated to include within his father's record, The Book of Mormon. (I use the large-sized 1888 edition with Apostle Orson Pratt's original footnotes, as they are far more reliable than the Talmage references that currently appear in all subsequent editions from 1920 on.)

(Ether 10:19-28) "And it came to pass that Lib also did that which was good in the sight of the Lord. And in the days of Lib the poisonous serpents were destroyed; wherefore they did go into the land southward [Pratt: South America], to hunt food for the people of the land, for the land was covered with animals of the forest. And Lib also himself became a great hunter. And they built a great city by the narrow neck of land, by the place where the sea divides the land. And they did preserve the land southward [Pratt: South America] for a wilderness, to get game. And the whole face of the land northward [Pratt: North America] was covered with inhabitants.

"And they were exceeding industrious, and they did buy and sell, and traffic one with another, that they might get gain. And they did work in all manner of ore, and they did make gold, and silver, and iron, and brass, and all manner of metals; and they did dig it out of the earth; wherefore they did cast up mighty heaps of earth to get ore, of gold, and of silver, and of iron, and of copper. And they did work all manner of fine work.

"And they did have silks, and fine-twined linens; and they did work all manner of cloth, that they might clothe themselves from their nakedness. And they did make all manner of tools [Pratt: agricultural machinery] to till the earth, both to plow and to sow, to reap and to hoe, and also to thresh. And they did make all manner of tools with which they did work their beasts. And they did make all manner of weapons of war. And they did work all manner of work of exceeding curious workmanship.

"And never could be a people more blessed than were they, and more prospered by the hand of the Lord. And they were in a land that was choice above all lands, for the Lord had spoken it."

[Ether 11:5-6]. "And it came to pass that the brother of Shiblom caused that all the prophets who prophesied of the destruction of the people should be put to death. And there was great calamity in all the land, for they had testified that a greater curse should come upon the land, and also upon the people, and that there should be a great destruction among them, such an one as never had been upon the face of the earth; and their bones should become as heaps of earth [Pratt: The ancient mounds of North America] upon the face of the land, except they should repent of their wickedness."

Elder George Reynolds of the First Quorum of the Seventy eloquently captured the unsurpassed glory of earth's mightiest ancient empire in *The Story of The Book of Mormon* (Salt Lake City: Joseph Hyrum Parry, 1888, pp. 451-452): "The contemporary nations on the eastern continent – Egypt, Chaldea and Babylonia – were insignificant when compared with the vast extent of territory held and filled by the Jaredites. They were the sole rulers of the whole Western Hemisphere, and possibly the originals, whence arose the stories of the greatness and grandeur of the fabled Atlantis. For we have no account in the sacred records that God shut them out from the knowledge of the rest of mankind when he planted them in America, as he afterwards did the Nephites. And late research has shown that the geographical knowledge of the ancients was much greater in the earlier ages than at the time of the Savior and a few hundred years previous to his advent."

When the truth someday becomes fully known among a generation of Millennial Saints more righteous and believing than their predecessors were, then ALL of the records belonging to this particular race will finally show the complete extent of their power and influence in the ancient world. I have already seen some of those records and pictures on numerous artifacts formerly placed in an old burial chamber of a huge king and his equally large queen, located in the mountains somewhere between Manti and Ephraim, Sanpete County, in south-central Utah. And they show that the Jaredites colonized areas extending from the frozen regions of Canada's northernmost provinces to the equally frigid and desolate wastes of Chile's most bottom extreme outpost at Tierra del Fuego, as well as from the Pacific to Atlantic coasts.

Their ships sailed further and reached more distant lands than either the Phoenicians or later Vikings combined. They influenced the world in ways we can't even imagine, giving inspiration to those fledgling societies that sprung up in Egypt, India, and China shortly after the human dispersion that followed the Tower of Babel's destruction. Fireworks, the alphabet, silk weaving, glass-blowing, lacquer varnish, a calendrical system, sophisticated metallurgy, and monumental architecture are but a few of their contributions to which the rest of the world owes a great debt.

And the physical evidence for most of this was neatly compacted a couple of millenniums ago in a few forgotten chambers that stand as silent museums waiting to be discovered, with only God's holy angels as their sole curators and caretakers.

CHAPTER FOURTEEN

LOOKING FOR THE FORTUNES OF EXTINCT EMPIRES

In the intervening years since the Manti mummy caves and John Brewer created considerable stir, and like an old itch that won't go away, the stray mutts of the archaeological world scratched here and there in hopes of some relief. Dr. Jesse Jennings of the U. of U. passed away with what little bit of ferocity was left in him, and Dr. Ray Matheny of BYU was last seen heading out those institutional doors to quieter pastures of leisure retirement. Paul Cheesman died some years ago of cancer and his wife Millie was artfully persuaded into donating most of his huge collection dealing with ancient artifacts to Brigham Young University in Provo, where it now securely languishes in the Special Collections section of the Lee Library under lock and key. And following a number of unfortunate setbacks (including the tragic death of one of his sons), John Brewer experienced declining memory failure and saw his former exuberant vitality for ancient things dwindle away into a hazy mist of clouded and confused recollections.

These days, though, there appears to be a "new breed" of relic hunters on the horizon who practice what I like to call "alternative archaeology." As Brad Eatchell of Salt Lake City and Steve Shaffer of Spanish Fork so adroitly put it: "We go out to hunt up these things for fun and pleasure. It isn't our purpose to make money off them, for none of the things we've found are for sale. And while we may confer with some of the Brethren occasionally [in this case, with Elder Robert E. Wells of the First Quorum of The Seventy concerning some recent Manti plate finds of their own], we try to steer clear of BYU's Department of Archaeology, F.A.R.M.S. and Hugh Nibley. From the experience of others, we've learned that there is a healthy dose of skepticism about anything ancient being discovered. They seem to have the attitude that if an artifact isn't found by one of their kind, then it isn't worth examining and can't be authentic." (Based on oral interviews with both men, in person on May 20th and again by phone on May 30th, 2000. In each case, this author typed out exactly what they said and then read it back to them for any necessary readjustments, in order to be able to quote them correctly.)

In a recent visit, they showed me some remarkable artifacts bearing ancient inscriptions similar to those that have appeared on many metal plates taken out of the two Jaredite treasure caves in Sanpete County in times past. How they came about finding them is an interesting story in and of itself. They were accompanied by Brad's father, Wesley Eatchel. Here is their story just as they told it to me some time ago.

"In August 1998, the three of us were down in Dodge Canyon in Sanpete Valley, which lays about 7.5 miles directly west of the Manti Temple, and on the extreme south end of the Sanpitch Mountains. We were there for the sole purpose of investigating the canyon, because BYU archaeologists had gone in there before us and flagged certain points of interest to them with little blue pennants. We brought along a good metal detector with which we started scanning the ground. We soon located an ancient building foundation that had been made of dressed stone arranged in a square pattern.

"The machine emitted a steady beep-beep indicating the presence of metal somewhere beneath one particular cornerstone. Once we got it removed, we noticed a cavity or hollow depression off to one side. One of us [Steve Shaffer] decided to take the risk of bending down and gingerly sticking his hand into the hole, hoping and praying all the while that there was no rattlesnake curled up inside.

"Steve's hand touched something made of metal and he carefully withdrew a couple of small metal plates. We cleaned the dirt away and discovered some ancient hieroglyphics inscribed on their surfaces. We were astonished by the similarity which these characters bore to those on the Brewer plates. We took them back to Spanish Fork and had a professional geologist and epigraphic specialist examine them. A spectographic analysis showed the plates to be primarily composed of galena alloy, which is a lead-and-silver mix in combination with a few other trace elements. Our inscription authority was a past president of the Utah State Epigraphic Society. He brought along some documents

Brad Eatchell holding the two galena plates with Jaredite inscriptions that were obtained from an excavation directly west of the Manti Temple and on the south end of the Sanpitch Mountains.

These inscripted plates recently excavated in Sanpete County bear astonishingly similar characters to those found on the Brewer plates, which suggests that the same ancient culture wrote both, though probably in different time periods.

from his own archives that showed a variation of ancient language characters from Celtic, Iberic, Phoenician and old Libyan. We found about a dozen characters on our two plates that matched up perfectly with some of these others. Though we never got any kind of interpretation from this as to the plates' messages, we both felt that these other languages could have been influenced by the ancient Jaredites through possible contact in some way."

Both men are respected within their own community circles and thought of as being "reasonable fellows with above-average intelligence," according to several close friends and neighbors. Brad Eatchell works for The Church of Jesus Christ of Latter-day Saints in its mapping department and is responsible for making any new boundary changes that affect wards, stakes, and missions throughout the world somewhere. Steve Shaffer is retired from Geneva Steel in Orem and has been relic hunting for a number of years now; he is the author of several popular books on lost mines and buried treasures.

Another of those who periodically practices this form of "alternative archaeology" is Terry Carter of Orem. A licensed electrician by trade, he has investigated a number of different sites in the West and even in Mexico, some of which have turned up modestly surprising yields for him. He begs to differ with the other two men in his approach to things: "I'm a blue-collar worker still trying to make ends meet. I go relic hunting when I have a little time because of my interest in such things. I find it very relaxing to do. I don't believe that anything found should ever be sold." (Oral interview in person with Terry Carter at his home in Orem, Utah on May 21st, 2000.)

The late summer of 1931 found my grandfather Jacob Heinerman, Sr. and my dad (also Jacob Heinerman) jointly operating a small family-owned moving business in downtown Salt Lake City. They usually parked outside the Occidental Saloon which was then situated at 16 East 100 South. A hand-printed cardboard sign stuck in the passenger side front window read, "Moving & Express." Some of their regular customers or anyone else in need of moving services would call down to the Occidental and ask for Jake, Sr. or Jake, Jr. One of the bartenders would walk out and notify them of such incoming phone calls. One or the other would go inside and retrieve such messages.

On a particular Thursday morning of August 6th, 1931, a call came in for them to travel northward to Ogden to pick up a piano which had just arrived by train from the East and deliver it to a certain location in another town just a few miles further up the road. They pulled into the big Slade Moving & Transfer warehouse in Ogden a couple of hours later. My father, as a young man, remembers looking up and seeing a huge sign marked in big bold letters that read, "The World Moves & So Does Slade." They loaded the heavy crated musical instrument on the back of their 1931 Model T truck and proceeded north to Brigham City, the final point of delivery.

There they met up with a prominent local architect by the name of Chris Simonsen. He had just designed and built an elegant home for a rich family and had been asked to help with some of the interior decorating. He suggested that a lovely grand piano in the drawing room would add a special touch to the place; his idea was readily accepted and an order placed for such a fine but enjoyable furnishing.

Following this delivery job, Simonsen (also a former city mayor in that locale) invited both Heinermans to join him for lunch at a popular eatery, The Paris Café. While waiting for their food to arrive and during the course of the meal itself, he entertained them with some of the early history of the place gleaned from some of the old-timers in Box Elder County.

My dad, who was then 17 years of age at the time, found one story, in particular, to be especially interesting to him. Oddly enough though, my grandfather, who was a strict convert and stuck primarily with the basic gospel fundamentals, didn't give the tale much credence. He and my father discussed it at some length upon their return to Salt Lake City. While my dad kept an open mind and believing heart on the matter, grandpa simply dismissed it as "imagined hearsay" and left it at that.

Some 69 years later, my father, now an active octogenarian, vividly recalls the more important details of what Brigham City's ex-mayor told him and his dad that Thursday afternoon of August 6th, 1931 in The Paris Café over a hearty lunch. The following narrative about treasure caves in Utah's remote southern wilderness is taken from my father's own verbal recollection as well as his written, unpublished memoirs contained within one volume of my many, extensive journals.

Sometime during 1911, an old and prominent pioneer figure by the name of Amos Wright came down from Bennington, Bear Lake County, Idaho with two of his grown sons to the Merrill Lumber Co. in Brigham City, where Chris Simonsen kept his architect's office. Wright had been the ward bishop of this small farming community just north of Montpelier for a number of years. As a teenager he mastered the Shoshone language, which later proved very useful during several church missions that he served among these Indian people. By the time he was 21 years old, Wright had served as an Indian translator, a freighter, a Pony Express rider, church missionary, and general adventurer.

(Though this wasn't a part of the story which Simonsen shared with the Heinermans, it should be mentioned here in passing, at least, that this was the same Amos Wright who tended Church cattle over one winter near Portage at the request of Apostle Lorenzo Snow but was never paid for his services. And when he finally did approach Elder Snow in the street on the matter sometime later, the other claimed he was in a hurry to make an appointment on time and refused to stop and talk. Whereupon, the young and impetuous Wright tackled the older Church leader around his waist and threw him to the ground. He reached inside the older man's coat pocket, helped himself to whatever money was available and left without even bothering to help the Apostle get up. He gave the money to his wife to buy some needful things for their newborn, but said nothing about the incident. A little over a week later, Wright received a letter in the mail announcing his formal excommunication from the Church of Jesus Christ of Latter-day Saints. It took six years, the loss of a child, and some serious repentance before he was rebaptized and reconfirmed into full fellowship again. Another 17 years were to follow before Lorenzo Snow expressed his sincere apologies for the rude treatment he had given Wright in Brigham City. Both men shed tears of joy, hugged each other, and renewed their friendship forever. For more details, see Geneva E. Wright's book on *Amos Wright: Mormon Frontiersman* (Provo: Council Press, 1981; pp. 68-70;105;205-206.)

Wright and his sons were at the lumber yard for several hours. While they took their time in loading some rough-cut dimensional material into the big wagon they brought with them, Wright and Simonsen engaged in a delightful conversation on a variety of topics. Being keenly interested in knowing more about the early history of

Utah, the architect pressed the old bishop into telling him incidents from his own early life.

Amos recounted an episode which must have transpired shortly after he gave up riding as a mail courier for the Pony Express. He accompanied two friends about his own age to their homes in Kanab in the southern part of the state. Here he met the famed buckskin "Apostle to the Lamanites" Jacob Hamblin, who shared a most intriguing tale with Wright and a few other select men one night at the home of Ira Hatch.

Hamblin opened up the conversation by noting that people sometimes had questioned him on why he did so many things among the Lamanites without first consulting with the Church Authorities in Salt Lake City. His standard reply to them always was that while Church President Brigham Young had called and set him apart as a special Apostle to the Indians, he actually took his regular "marching orders" from the Three Nephites of The Book of Mormon fame. (These were three of the original twelve Disciples whom Jesus Christ appointed to preside over His Church which He established in the Western Hemisphere, in the northern part of Colombia, shortly after His Resurrection. While nine eventually died of old age, three were given the unique blessing of having their physical bodies undergo special changes which enabled them to continue living for many, many centuries without ever growing old and possessing powers similar to those of resurrected angels. In this form, they could come and go as they pleased throughout the earth and even visit other inhabited planets and moons in this solar system, if they so desired. They would also no longer be subject to diseases or temptations from the Evil One. These Three Nephites are the most prominent characters in early Mormon folklore of the 19th century. The best study ever done on this cultural phenomena is ethnologist Hector Lee's 1947 doctoral dissertation for the University of New Mexico entitled, *The Three Nephites: The Substance and Significance of the Legend in Folklore*.)

Anyhow, Hamblin was visited upon one particular occasion by two of these Three Nephites. They invited him to accompany them into the great stretch of wilderness expanse directly south of Kanab. (At this point in his narrative ex-mayor Simonsen paused long enough to point out to my granddad and father that when Bishop Wright rehearsed the affair to him, he emphasized that Hamblin claimed it only took them less than an hour to make this historic journey. And although Hamblin never actually stated it as such, he left the distinct impression with his listeners that his physical conveyance to the spot which he was taken, was done through some kind of supernatural power.)

Hamblin apparently didn't think it was important enough or pertinent to his story, to disclose details about the physical appearances of his two semi-immortal hosts. Hence, age, size, and manner of their dresses never entered into the telling of his most remarkable tale. The only attention given to detail was in regard to the place they visited. While not entirely specific (probably for sworn secrecy reasons), the "buckskin apostle" alluded to the immediate area of their visit as being somewhere near the southern Utah and northern Arizona border "below Kanab a distance and in Indian country."

One of his hosts informed him that (at that time) no human had set foot on the ground which they were then standing for a number of centuries! He then stretched forth his hand in front of a large, natural rock wall facing them and an entry way became promptly apparent. (Whether a particular stone actually rolled aside for this purpose was never mentioned. As to exactly how this was done remains a mystery.)

The three of them went inside, one Nephite leading the way, Hamblin in the middle, and his companion bringing up the rear. The inside seemed to be rather high, wide, and deep. Hamblin used the word "cavern" several times to describe what the room resembled to him. Everything about it seemed to have been naturally formed instead of bearing man-made signs of expansion or finishing.

Sunlight from outside was swallowed up by a softer brilliance of illumination from within. But as to the source of the internal lightning, Hamblin was never told. His footsteps were directed towards the back part of one section of a limestone wall, against which were stacked numerous stone boxes of varying descriptions. In each of them, he was told by one of his hosts, were contained metallic plates representing the two great ancient cultures which inhabited the Americas several thousand years ago. Inscribed on them were the many histories, prophecies, wars, and general activities of the Jaredites (who came from the Tower of Babel) and their own people (the Nephites), who came from Jerusalem at the time of King

Nebuchadnezzar's invasion and subsequent conquest of that city and adjacent land.

Hamblin remained still and said nothing, undoubtedly quite awestruck with what he saw. His informant said that these records had been gathered together in that particular spot over a period of time by divine means, from former places of secretion in other parts of the Americas (presumably from North, Central and South America). And that the time would come when they would be brought forth by designated servants of the Most High and eventually translated into English through the gift and power of God. These would then become the scriptures for all those living during the Millennium, when Satan would be bound for a thousand years and there would be no more wickedness on earth during that time.

The first of those to be translated would be the Brass Plates (frequently mentioned in the Book of Mormon). They would give a true account of everything which happened from the very beginning of time down to the time of the prophet Jeremiah. What was contained on them would be a much more complete record than what is presently found in the Old Testament. Many of God's mysteries and workings would then become more abundantly manifested, including many things that happened before the Flood, as well as afterwards.

The entire genealogy and true origins of the Lamanites (or Native Americans) would also be provided. And with this valuable information, an even greater missionary work would then be done among the remnants of these people scattered over the Americas. Such would become the means of leading the more faithful among them into the Restored Gospel, thereby making them a great and powerful people!

Hamblin was promised that he would be an active participant in these events but not in his present flesh (presumably as a resurrected being). Other things were shown and told to him which he could not divulge. But he closed his thrilling tale in the home of Ira Hatch that particular night before an obviously astonished but very small audience, with his testimony. Bishop Wright told Simonsen that when he heard Hamblin's concluding remarks, it seemed to him as if there were a fire welling up inside of him that could not be contained. Hamblin looked around the room with a steady fix on everyone's eyes and soberly declared that ALL the records from which the Book of

Mormon had been compiled were safely hid away and well guarded some good distance from where they all resided. He said he had seen these things with his own eyes and heard this report from two of the Three Nephites themselves. He then bore a powerful testimony of the Book of Mormon itself and admonished everyone in that room to read every word and live by its precepts.

When the old bishop finished, Simonsen said that he felt a peculiar feeling creep over him that he couldn't effectively describe. He told the older and younger Heinermans that it wasn't bad, just odd and different. After that, Amos Wright said no more on the subject and acted as if he didn't want to talk about it anymore. The meaning of it then held greater purpose in the young architect's life than later after he entered into business and politics. But Simonsen still considered the episode something more than just a mere novelty, although he wasn't going to stake his testimony on that alone.

My grandfather and dad clearly understood the terms on which this highly unusual story had come to them. It was third-hand and not from the original source itself. And with each retelling came slight but unintentional variations and changes. The German convert from the Old Country insisted to his son on their way back to Salt Lake City later that afternoon, that if there was anything at all to this (which he didn't think there was), that it would come through the proper channels of the Church in its own appointed time and to no one else. He was very adamant with his son in this matter.

After my aged father had explained this singular event from his youth in his usual calm and dignified style, he paused to think a few moments on whatever commentary he would be giving it for my benefit. Finally, after some lapse of consideration, he made several wise observations. First, he felt that his own father had been unduly biased in the expression of his own feelings on the subject. Dad reminded me that his father didn't even believe that Joseph Smith lived plural marriage, although LDS Church history is replete with evidence to the contrary. He only used this example to show just how strongly opinionated my grandfather had been in his life.

Secondly, my dad had always felt ever since hearing Simonsen's narrative, that it was based in truth. The problem, though, he correctly noted is just how much was truth and how much was hearsay gleaned from the periodic retelling of the same. Only the Holy

Spirit could confirm that within one's own soul after taking this issue up with the Lord in fervent prayer. Dad had received his own knowledge about this, but felt it was not for public consumption in a book like this. But he encouraged me to write up the incident just as he had related it and also previously referred to in his written history contained within one of my earlier journals.

As further evidence of this unique visit, my father got up from his chair and slowly ambled over to his antique secretary desk. After some momentary shuffling of papers, he produced a faded menu taken from the diner on which he had scribbled some of the highlights to Simonsen's intriguing tale. I handled the curious souvenir with a little reverence as I read dad's notations on the subject. It only re-verified what I already knew to be true, because my father has never been in the habit of lying, having set for himself an unprecedented record of honesty in all of his transactions that is certainly very worthy of emulation.

CHAPTER FIFTEEN

AN ELEMENT OF DANGER TO RELIC WORK

Those who've been specially privileged to uncover sacred records or become involved with ancient burial treasure sites, know all too well their joy and excitement engendered from the things they've found is apt to also be tinged with the anxiety and unhappiness induced by an assortment of dangers always lurking near. This was true of the Prophet Joseph Smith and anyone else so singularly blessed. LDS Apostle George Q. Cannon spelled out what some of these fearful elements were for the young prophet in his classic biography *The Life of Joseph Smith The Prophet* (Salt Lake City: The Deseret News Press, 1907; pp. 23-26):

"[The Angel] Moroni disappeared, and THE PROPHET OF THE LAST DISPENSATION stood upon [the Hill] Cumorah, clasping to his bosom the priceless trust [consisting of the ring-bound Gold Plates and "an ancient breastplate of pure gold" to which was attached "two precious stones set in arch of silver" known as the Urim and Thummim].

"Joseph folded the golden record of past generations beneath his mantle and sped homeward. The words of Moroni had been prophetic; three different times in the brief journey to his house, the chosen minister of salvation was assailed by unknown men – emissaries of the Evil One, who sought to strike him to the earth and rob him of his precious charge. Once they dealt him a terrific blow with a bludgeon, but he did not fall. He was a man of rare physical endowments, yet on this occasion his own strength and activity, without the help of the Lord, would not have delivered him or been sufficient to cast his assailants one by one prone in the dust with the irresistible force which he used against them. With the plates unharmed, but himself bruised, and panting from the contest, Joseph reached his home.

"After this important hour, the powers of darkness arrayed all their subtle and murderous influences against him. Abominable false-hoods were cunningly circulated against himself and his father's family, the purpose being to excite the rage of the populace against them. Constantly the Prophet's life was beset by assassins; the sacred record was sought by robbers. Each hour brought some new menace. Men, lurking by his pathway, discharged deadly weapons at his person; and mobs attacked him and invaded his home. Wherever the plates were supposed to be hidden, there were the despoilers breaking through bolts and walls. Open force failing, subtle stratagems were devised for the destruction of the Prophet's life and the abstraction of the plates.

"These numerous efforts all failed to accomplish the ends at which they were aimed. But they prevented Joseph from obtaining the safe leisure necessary for his labor of translation. Anxious to pursue his heaven-appointed work without the interruption of these continued attacks, he was let to the idea of removing from Manchester. Personal fear was not an element of his nature, and no selfish motive prompted his resolve; but in no other visible manner could his sacred instructions be fulfilled. The home of [his wife] Emma's parents in Susquehanna County, Pennsylvania, was the place which he selected, and thither he determined to journey [to the now extinct but ironi-cally-named hamlet of Harmony].

"But Satan was not idle. Twice while on the journey was the servant of God stopped by officers, who, under a pretended warrant of law, searched his wagon for plates, but the Angel of the Lord blinded the eyes of the wicked and they found not what they sought. For the succeeding sixteen or seventeen years from the time of which we write his steps were beset by peril. Violence and murder lurked in his pathway. He was never free from menace. His was a stormy career; but he was amply qualified for it."

Though John Brewer and I were never involved with things as precious and sacred as the Gold Plates and Urim and Thummim, yet the ancient Jaredite relics that we shared a knowledge in together, brought upon us a great deal of trouble from sources we never imag-ined possible. Snakes, both the slithering as well as legged kind, happened to be one major factor. I remember one time in mid-Summer when Brewer and I left the old cave via his long crawl tunnel. Not too far from the tunnel entrance, I heard Brewer shout at the top of his lungs, "Oh [expletive], a rattlesnake!" He immediately started pushing himself backwards in a great hurry, which necessitated me doing the same likewise or else run the risk of getting kicked in the head with his feet. He retrieved one of the javelins from the main treasure chamber and using this implement in front of him managed to push the snake out of the tunnel once we attempted a second exit.

A disaffected Church member by the name of Robert Hunt Simmons had "immersed himself in Indian history [and] staked out mining claims on an island in the Great Salt Lake, where he was convinced there were precious metals, artifacts, and a lost civilization to be found." In the due process of time, some of his claims and eventual finds attracted the interest of the since-deceased, murderous cult leader Ervil LeBaron and his polygamous Church of the Lamb of God. Assuming the alias of Ellery Steelson, the over-confident Ervil ingratiated himself with the Simmons, persuading the mentally unstable man to join forces with Ervil's cult. Upon discovering Steelson's true identity, Simmons wrote a blistering note to LeBaron, calling his "revelations from the darker regions," and openly challenged Ervil's presumed power and authority as the "One Mighty and Strong" spoken of in holy writ (see Doctrine & Covenants 85:7). This letter so enraged Ervil that he assigned three of his top thugs to "bump off" Simmons in the high desert plateau country just south of Price, UT; they lured the unsuspecting man to his death on the pretense of going to look for "an old Nephite or Jaredite treasure vault," before blowing the back of his head off with a sawed-off 12 gauge shotgun (see Ben Bradlee's and Dale Van Atta's *Prophet of Blood: the Untold Story of Ervil LeBaron and The Lambs of God* (New York: G. P. Putnam's Sons, 1981; pp. 181-190).

Ervil LeBaron was one of seven brothers, the other being Joel (whom he assassinated over a cultic power dispute), Verlan, Alma, Floren, Ben, and, last but not least, Ross LeBaron of Cane Beds, Arizona. Ross had settled along the Utah-Arizona strip some years ago in the belief that much of the wealth of the ancient Book of Mormon peoples, such as the Jaredites and Nephites, had been purposely secreted at different sites in this vast area of desert wilderness straddling both states. For years he and his cohorts had been on numerous treasure digs all over the region but always meeting with failure.

Therefore, it came as no surprise when Ervil's highly-imaginative brother and a few others journeyed northward to Sanpete County upon hearing about some of the purported riches taken from the old cave by Mr. Brewer. Ross met with him in private and the next thing I knew John was introducing me to one of the infamous LeBaron brothers. I was flabbergasted beyond belief that Brewer could be so naive and careless as to do this, considering how cautious he had been before with others and especially with myself until I had earned his complete confidence. LeBaron wanted to know more about the second cave, in particular, something that John and I had always kept to ourselves and never divulged to anyone. Yet, here now, this stranger knew intimate things connected with the treasure site high in the mountains a little south of Wales that only Brewer and I were privy to.

To say that I was angry at John for his stupidity and gullibility is an understatement. I fairly seethed with boiling emotions and once we managed to get rid of Ross for the time being, I vented my full spleen upon Brewer. I asked him, "How could you be so damned dumb in telling this guy anything about the second cave?" Brewer shrugged his shoulders and quietly admitted that he already knew he had made a big mistake, for "an angel of God told me so before you arrived" at the Moroni Sewage Treatment Plant (where John then worked). I repeatedly asked him why he had volunteered such sensitive information to such a clan member from a potentially dangerous family. He gave my question some thought before muttering that it was probably to bolster his ego, if nothing else, in order to appear more important in the stranger's eyes.

Then and there it finally dawned on me that most of the trouble Brewer had to endure in the years preceding our getting together, were pretty much of his own making. I now fully understood something I should have earlier in the relationship, and that was the man's own insecurity and flagging self-confidence. In a way, Brewer is no different than any of us when it comes to the need to be recognized and appreciated for who you are and your efforts in life. I can't fault a person for wanting this, but the way in which John had been going about it was all wrong. He was like a little kid in grade school when they used to have "Show and Tell"– every child would bring something interesting to school and then stand up when it was his or her turn and show it to the rest of the class and then tell a little about it. Brewer never really grew up in this sense, for the little child in him had kept this version of "Show and Tell" going for many years with a lot of people in regards to his spectacular finds. The key to this personality puzzle was a fairly innocuous statement which Brewer quietly made one time in passing: "Without this cave and the things in it, I would be a nobody!" He, indeed, somebody important with these artifacts.

It wasn't long after Brewer's unwise tip-off to Ross LeBaron about the second cave, that some followers of his wicked brother Ervil darkened our doorsteps in Moroni and Manti. Brewer claimed that one of his daughters was physically threatened on her way home from school, while over in my neck of the wood, an anonymous phone call to my father and brother rattled their mental cages pretty good.

On one of several trips to the cave I retreived a box that weighed approximately 50 lbs.

Brewer and I eventually cut away the vegetative covering on the box and were quite intrigued with its unusual design patterns. We saw bits and pieces of Hopi and Maya cultures in the themes thereon depicted. And yet we knew it was still of Jaredite origin, only from a much later era (probably when some war survivors made contact with the Mulekites somewhere in the Yucatan Peninsula). (For the uninformed, the Mulekites were one of three distinctive cultural groups mentioned in the Book of Mormon to emigrate to the Americas in ancient times. First came the Jaredites from the Tower of Babel via the Yellow Sea and the North Pacific Ocean to the west coast of Mexico; probably near present-day Acapulco. Then came the Nephites and the Mulekites out of Jerusalem between 599 and 588 B.C., each taking separate routes of travel to the New World—the former reached Valparaiso, Chile in South America via the Arabian Sea, Indian Ocean and the South Pacific, while the latter went via the Mediterranean Sea, the North Atlantic Ocean and the Caribbean Sea to somewhere around the Yucatan Peninsula in eastern Mexico. Both groups eventually met each other a few centuries later in Columbia in the extreme northwestern part of the South American continent, where they united into a single nation. The Nephites, having brought with them across the ocean metallic records giving a history of their forefathers and being a highly educated people, taught the descendants of the Mulekites (now called the people of Zarahemla after their ruler) these things, since the latter never brought any records with them and were without a written history of any kind.)

After carefully opening this highly-decorative, stuccoed stone box, we were both very surprised by what we found inside. In similar boxes of varying sizes we had carried from the older burial chamber near Manti and from this naturally-formed cave by Wales, there would always be found numbers of loose metallic plates usually cushioned by thin layers of dried, shredded vegetative matter of some sort. But imagine our astonishment when we lifted off the cover of this particular box, retrieved by myself at great risk, and found inside not only wonderfully inscribed plates made of gold alloy, but also a long, slender rod measuring about 14 inches long and slightly over one-quarter inch in diameter, and made entirely of pure gold!

It was decided, for security reasons, to take this particular box to my family's home in Manti, Utah where it was kept for safe-keeping. Brewer and I were sufficiently intrigued by these particular contents that our amazement over them held for several days before gradually waning. Since neither of us could understand the inscriptions on any of the plates we had found in our periodic visits to both caves, there were no clues offered as to what the rod signified. Stranger still, one of the gold plates with it contained only a few brief inscriptions and a number of curved line drawings with some curious coordinates that Brewer enthusiastically proclaimed was a map to more buried treasure!

I withheld judgment on this last pronouncement and decided to adopt a more conservative "wait-and-see" attitude, which I felt was the wiser course to follow. Brewer had always been enamored with inscribed plates, especially those made of gold alloy. Though he never admitted to it, I believed in my heart that he was charmed by their rich-looking appearance. So it was decided by himself, of course, that he would keep the stone box and most of its contents; but he graciously consented for me to retain the one gold map plate and the solid gold rod that seemed to go with it. I didn't let on that I knew this, but instinct indicated they were a perfectly matched pair.

Not long after this, events in both our lives took sudden turns for the worst in terms of our previously perfect relationship. The things connected with our sudden and explosive breakup need not be mentioned here for the world to know about. God alone knows who was at fault and who tried to remain faithful to the disintegrating friendship. Suffice it to say, though, the one who had formerly prayed

A natural entrance to a mountainous cave that is fairly typical of the one situated high up and to the southwest of Wales, Utah. The entrance way to the real cave is so well hidden that unless someone was generally acquainted with the area, that person could look all day long and walk in many circles without finding it. There were no mummies interred within its chambers that we could tell. But there were a great deal more stone boxes filled with numerous records than existed in the first cave. Brewer suggested, though without any geological evidence to back it up, that this second cave continued for miles beneath the mountains and came out on the other side somewhere just below Levan on State Road 28.

that someone else trustworthy enough would eventually be brought to him, ultimately suffered the worst in the whole affair. First, it was the tragic loss of his oldest son, secondly, his job, and finally, his mind lost much of its ability to reason clearly.

When I inquired of my wise father as to the proper disposal of those things which had been previously removed from the cave by myself and Brewer and had been committed into my care by the man, my father made this fair recommendation: "If Brewer ever asks for their return, then surrender them ALL without protest. In the meantime, though, keep them safely secreted and be very careful to whom you show them." Over two decades have passed and I have diligently followed his counsel: Brewer never again contacted me and I became exceedingly stingy and overly cautious with whom I shared these sacred treasures.

And what about that solid gold rod and metal map of gold alloy which was found in that ancient stone box removed from one of the treasure caves by myself some years ago? Ah, well my friend that is intended for another time and, who knows, probably meant for another book later on.

The stone box that was retrieved from the second cave near Wales, Utah. Notice the Maya-looking features on the heads of those side portraits depicted here. And no, the long curlicues adorning their scalps are *not* suggestive of alien antennaes, but possibly bird tail feathers or even individual hair strands gussied up with wax or oil for cultural reasons.

The portrayal of a ship with extended oars demonstrates that the Jaredites conducted extensive sailing forays among themselves and with outside groups for unsolicited gains, trade purposes, and exploration. The male figure shown here assuming what seems to be a dance position, could very well have been a Jaradite priest or holy man of some sort. The wing spread emanating from his back could also just as easily infer an angelic being from Heaven. In fact, the whole image itself brings to mind what a Hopi shaman might employ in some kind of ceremonial ritual or dance.

209

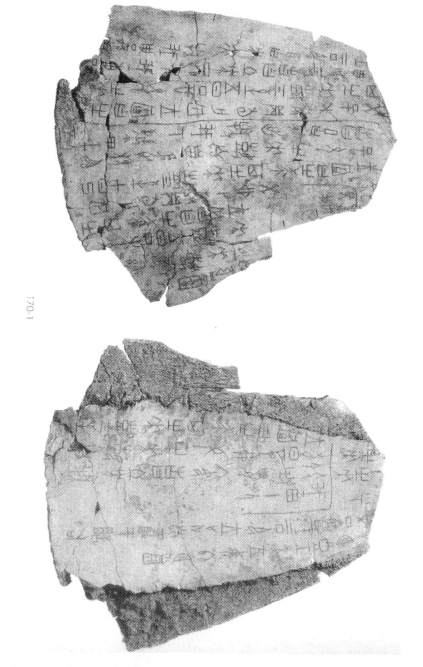

Large ox bone with oracle inscriptions in vermillion. Discovered in Anyang, Henan Province, mainland China. Inscribed during the Shang Dynasty sometime in the 13th century B.C.

Closeup of the same inscriptions (Circa 13th century B.C., Shang
Dynasty, mainland China).

Large ox bone with oracle inscription, made during Shang Dynasty (sometime in 13th century B.C. and discovered in Anyang, Hanan Province. A total of 150,000 oracle bones have come to light containing 5,000-odd characters, over 4,000 of which are legible.

Inscriptions on sacrificial ceremony and hunting with characters somewhat wimilar in style to the Jaredite inscriptions on the Brewer metal plates found in an ancient burial cave near Manti, Utah.

Closeup of the same inscriptions (compare these with some of the Jaredite inscriptions on the Brewer plates in the pages following this. Oracle bone contents touched on various aspects of Shang society: class relations, armed forces, and corporal punishment; agriculture, animal husbandry, hunting, handicrafts, trade and communications; astronomy, the calender and medicine; worship of the Celestial Ruler, nature and ancestors.

Gold, copper, brass, and lead plates from an ancient burial tomb near Manti, Sanpete Co., in southcentral Utah. Vegetative materials found in various stone boxes from which these plates were recovered, have been dated to around 1200 B.C. The inscriptions are very similar in some ways to those found on ancient oracle bones of about the same time period in mainland China.

(see last caption)

216

(see last caption)